מסורה

ArtScroll Series®

Rabbi Nosson Scherman / Rabbi Meir Zlotowitz

General Editors

Ideas and stories
to keep you going
when you're happy
and pick you up
when you're down

Over 100 teenage girls
share their stories

Published by
Mesorah Publications, ltd

More

GIFTS
-for-
TEENS

Roiza D. Weinreich

FIRST EDITION
First Impression … November 2004

Published and Distributed by
MESORAH PUBLICATIONS, LTD.
4401 Second Avenue / Brooklyn, N.Y 11232

Distributed in Europe by
LEHMANNS
Unit E, Viking Business Park
Rolling Mill Road
Jarow, Tyne & Wear, NE32 3DP
England

Distributed in Australia and New Zealand by
GOLDS WORLDS OF JUDAICA
3-13 William Street
Balaclava, Melbourne 3183
Victoria, Australia

Distributed in Israel by
SIFRIATI / A. GITLER — BOOKS
6 Hayarkon Street
Bnei Brak 51127

Distributed in South Africa by
KOLLEL BOOKSHOP
Shop 8A Norwood Hypermarket
Norwood 2196, Johannesburg, South Africa

Typography by CompuScribe at ArtScroll Studios, Ltd.
Printed in the United States of America by Noble Book Press Corp.
Bound by Sefercraft, Quality Bookbinders, Ltd., Brooklyn N.Y. 11232

לזכר נשמת

הרב שלום בן שרגא ברוך ווינדרייך ז"ל
Harav Sholom ben Shraga Baruch ז"ל

Each hour of his life overflowed
with energy, optimism,
kindness to others and determination
to serve Hashem and help Torah causes.

Many who have suffered in life express
dissatisfaction and resentment, but
his attitude was different.
As a Holocaust survivor his credo was,
"Life is so precious. Let's not waste it grumbling
and griping; let's enjoy every moment
and give joy to others."

תנצב"ה

Table of Contents

Acknowledgments

I would like to thank the many people who provided ideas and support during the process of writing this book:

Mrs. Ethel Gottlieb was thorough yet gentle while editing. Her insight and creative ideas added profoundly to the book. It was truly delightful and encouraging to work with her.

Gratitude goes to Rabbis Meir Zlotowitz and Nosson Scherman for putting their faith in this project and for their help in bringing about the impressive success of my previous books. My special thanks to Rabbi Sheah Brander whose expert knowledge and creativity made the book complete.

Thank you to Eli Kroen and Hershy Feuerwerker for a beautiful cover design. My appreciation to Mrs. Mindy Stern for proofreading, to Mrs. Tova Finkelman for her editorial comments, to Miss Esty Lebovits for her superb pagination, and to the entire ArtScroll staff. I consider it a privilege to participate in the ArtScroll Series.

My parents, Mr. and Mrs. Moshe Perlman and my mother-in-law Mrs. Pearl Weinreich have encouraged all my various undertakings. My husband Faivel patiently encouraged me not to give up when I faced minor setbacks.

I thank Hashem for the wide acceptance of my previous books and for the *zechus* to reach thousands of people around the world with Torah ideas that helped them to be better Jews.

וִיהִי נֹעַם ה׳ אֱלֹקֵינוּ עָלֵינוּ
וּמַעֲשֵׂה יָדֵינוּ כּוֹנְנָה עָלֵינוּ וּמַעֲשֵׂה יָדֵינוּ כּוֹנְנֵהוּ

May Hashem's presence and satisfaction rest upon us. May Hashem complete our efforts and assure their success. May the work of our hands establish Hashem's Kingdom on earth.

Introduction

How was this book born?

After A GIFT FOR TEENS was published, dozens of girls wrote to me and told me that the book helped them see things in new ways. Since the last book I've met dozens of teens just like you. I interviewed them by phone, observed them in person and read the letters and stories they so generously shared. I was drawn to these unsung heroines. Each one had a special nobility. Gradually my pile of stories grew. These stories made me smile and gave me hope. Therefore I wanted to share 200 new stories by teens with you. And so the sequel was born.

The girls you will meet in these stories have displayed simple wisdom, self-control and extraordinary kindness. Some had a valid reason to be miserable and yet they were not. Each of their accomplishments, no matter how small it may have appeared outwardly, was a personal triumph. Each new achievement gave them the encouragement to go further.

And the best part is that they are all ordinary teenagers like you. They challenged the attitudes that made them feel worthless and so can you.

Rabbi Samson Raphael Hirsh explains that a feeling of progression is synonymous with happiness, because the Hebrew word for happiness, *simchah*, is related to the word *tzemichah*, which means growth. We do not need to be finished to be fulfilled, we simply need to be on the way.

Imagine that you are standing at the corner, waiting for the tour bus to arrive. There is a wonderful feeling surging in you, the feeling that something good is about to happen.

This book is the tour bus; it will take you, the passenger, as far as you want to go.

The Gift
of Optimism
and Gratitude

Prove to Yourself That
You Are Capable

Attitude Check

Every once in a while someone asks me if there is such a thing as a born optimist. Consider the mood you are in right now. Can you describe it? What are you feeling? Do you want to experience life more completely? I have always wanted to prolong the times I was enjoying myself. I wanted to keep the memories of the celebrations in my life crystal clear. Another thing I have always wanted to do was to minimize the pain when I'm feeling down and to climb out of a rut quickly.

Have you perhaps been muttering, "Some people have a natural inclination to be optimistic but I'm just not that type"? These are the people you know who are relaxed and easygoing. They seem to be less sensitive. A joke is always on the tip of their tongue. Do you think that our moods are out of our control and that they simply come and go like the weather?

The truth is that you have a great degree of control over your thoughts and feelings. There are several techniques you will learn about in this book that will help you feel much better. If you have had many difficult struggles in the past, you will simply have to plan in advance for a positive experience now and in the future. By investing effort beforehand and focusing on the times you were positive and energetic, you will lay the foundation for days of joy and ease.

The purpose of the questionnaire that follows is to provide proof that you are capable. Even after several unsatisfactory experiences, success can reverse the unfavorable memories. With each additional successful day, you will feel more positive and will soon begin to spontaneously think optimistic thoughts from the first moment that you awake.

Remembering your good experiences helps you feel optimistic. When you perceive yourself as vulnerable because a problem has arisen, instead of worrying about the obstacles you will be facing, you can devote your full concentration to preparing for them. Knowing that you have managed stress well at other times helps you to be less sensitive and more flexible in meeting today's challenges. If you feel poised and confident before your day begins, the entire day is more pleasant.

Answer the questions below. Write the letter of the response that best describes how you feel.

1. How often do you think cheerful thoughts each day?
   a) hardly ever
   b) sometimes
   c) very often

2. How many times did you stop and smile today?

   a) hardly ever

   b) sometimes

   c) very often

3. When did you feel hopeful?

   a) morning

   b) evening

   c) throughout the day

4. How strong were your hopeful thoughts?

   a) mild

   b) moderate

   c) very intense

5. What other feelings accompanied your optimistic state?

   ☐ calmness   ☐ relaxation   ☐ humility

   ☐ closeness to Hashem   ☐ satisfaction   ☐ energy

   ☐ generosity   ☐ kindness

6. What did you do to sustain your hopeful feeling?

   a) continued with my routine

   b) gave *tzedakah*

   c) said a meaningful prayer

7. Were you feeling hopeful because:

   a) of a pleasant surprise

   b) a crisis had passed

   c) you noticed ordinary blessings

8. What did you conclude about your past success?

   a) I was lucky

   b) I was well prepared

   c) Hashem is kind

9. Define the word miracle:

   a) once-in-a-lifetime experience

   b) recovery from illness

   c) daily phenomena that show the Creator's plan and purpose

10. How long will you remember the good things happening to you?
    a) one day
    b) three days
    c) one or two weeks

11. What does this shape remind you of? (O)
    a) nothing
    b) an orange
    c) a person smiling

12. When you are working on a large project do you think about:
    a) how much you still must do
    b) how difficult the project is
    c) how much you've accomplished

To determine your score:
Give yourself 1 point for each A answer,
2 points for each B answer,
3 points for each C answer.
(For question 5, add 3 points. All choices are equally correct.)

Evaluating the Questionnaire

Score: 20 to 30:
You are probably an inspiration to others! You can view difficult situations as challenges instead of obstacles. This book should give you an even deeper perception of the optimistic attitude you already have.

10 to 20:
Congratulations! You have learned to take your stress in stride. You will probably want to apply the advice in this book to the specific aspects of your life that are difficult to handle.

0 to 10:
Like most people you have definite feelings of stress but you can still manage for weeks to avoid overwhelming situations. Don't worry about your problem areas. Congratulate yourself on your honesty about your feelings. When you complete the book, it will be encouraging to review these answers and see how you have grown.

How can I increase optimistic feelings right now?

It's important to bear in mind that you are close to serenity right now. Don't think about your worries. Don't fret over the past or feel anxious about the future. Simply choose to think of something beautiful instead. It takes only one moment to choose a lovely thought. That moment can change your attitude.

⁓⤳⬳

●◦ *Sunset*

*T*he busy day was drawing to a close. People at work were packing up after a long day. After shining all day the tired sun began to settle down. As a last good-bye, she displayed her prettiest colors.

The sun was a fiery orange. She emitted an array of color. The beautiful pastel shades gently spread over the vast sky. Pale lavender calmly blended into the azure blue. The orange faded into a serene cottony yellow. The clouds seemed plated with gold and angel-like. What a lovely way to say good-bye.

Miriam R.

⁓⤳⬳

●◦ *Musing at Sunset*

*T*he clear blue sky slowly tints as evening draws nearer. Purple lines streak the sky as the great ball of fire gradually sinks beneath the fluffy clouds.

The famous story of the woodcutter who always wanted to be something else comes to mind. He wanted to become the most powerful force in the world so he chose to become the sun. True, the sun is powerful.

It comes out in the spring melting away the last signs of winter and softly shines upon the flowers blooming so beautifully.

It happily shines on Pesach so that we can enjoy our holiday. It smiles at the children playing in the park.

In the summer it practically burns us, as it beats on us so strongly. As we lounge outside looking at the sun while sipping cold lemonade and licking ices, it watches us too.

As fall arrives and winter starts its gradual entry, the sun comes out less. The clouds and wind dominate. The sun is not as powerful.

The sun too must say goodnight. It always sends a colorful good-bye. Sunset reminds us of the Creator Who makes the sun shine. He also makes the winds blow and the clouds give rain. Everything is balanced. Everything is perfect.

Esty R.

Cultivating a Hopeful Attitude

Take a Few Moments to Savor Your Pleasant Memories

We were looking for an important phone number. We tried the telephone book. The number wasn't listed. A call to our cousin — who we knew had that number — didn't work either. The cousin wasn't home. I was beginning to feel impatient. I wanted to leave, but I needed the address and phone number. Then I turned to my daughter Chaya Rivky and said, "You saved their business card. It's in your *Baruch Hashem* book."

Chaya Rivky found her *Baruch Hashem* book and within minutes she had the telephone number. Once we had the book out we took a few moments to read some entries and to smile. This book was about four years old. The first entry that caught my eye was, "Rochel has two new teeth." I laughed; now Rochel is in Pre-1A. Then I read that someone got engaged. I was amazed because just yesterday I heard that this couple had a baby boy. I read about the first flowers of spring, a guest who came from out of town, and my daughter's friend whom she visited in New Jersey. It was a delight.

Do you sometimes hear a voice inside you that calls you to slow down?

Victory feels so good. Each day you face a mountain of tasks. At the end of the day if you've achieved your goal you feel like a winner. Yet tomorrow the new list of things to do might well be even longer. Do you sometimes hear your soul whisper that you've been running a marathon for too long? It's natural to feel discouraged.

Although you are getting many things done, your general situation doesn't feel any better. On the surface everything is glorious, but inside you there is a hole that no amount of possessions or assets can fill. When you forget the goals you've reached and the good things happening it creates a hole. Optimism is the magic ingredient that can fill that void. However, it is often overlooked in our complex lives.

In this murky, problem-filled world, it takes effort to find and preserve the golden moments of bliss. You have to look deeply. Find those small nuggets of enjoyment and look at them a second time. Don't just take a peek, look at your nugget intently. Optimism helps us connect with Hashem in every favorable detail of our ordinary life.

What made you smile today? Did you notice a butterfly hovering over a flower? Did you gaze up through the leaves of a tree and see the sunlight filter through? Did you hear a whisper and look up to see a robin hopping in your garden? Did your baby sister use a new word for the first time? Keep your smiles in a place where they won't be lost. Preserve your hopes and dreams. Guard your flashes of insight. Start looking for the feeble rays of sunlight that first break through the clouds. When you look for the light it becomes brighter.

Do problems cloud up your day?

Everyone has problems. Would it surprise you to learn that problems don't have to cloud up your feelings of hope? Difficulties need to be dealt with but simultaneously we must not let ourselves drown in a sea of problems. Optimism is our life raft. Simply taking a few minutes several times a day to count our blessings and view things in a favorable light can make a difference in our attitude. We all tend to magnify our problems by thinking about them without stopping. We even make problems worse by assuming that they are a reflection of our intellect and our talent.

Imagine these inner thoughts of a high school student who has just walked into class:

There is Baila sitting in the front seat all ready for class. She's so organized. She never panics because she always does her homework well in advance. Her notes are immaculate. I'm sure she doesn't have any problems. She's a genius.

Just look at me. I ran in at the last minute. I studied spelling, but yesterday the test was on the grammar section. I've totally run out of loose-leaf paper. If I pass it will be a miracle.

Such comparisons are not helpful. Yet that measuring stick always seems to be at the ready. Does it help us? I think not. Somehow we end up hitting ourselves with it.

You know better than anyone else that most of your daily worries are only temporary. Unfortunately, our daily opportunities to enjoy life also pass by quickly. So despite your problems decide that you will focus on the good things happening to you and thank Hashem.

How can you begin to take note of the good things happening in your life?

When I was in high school (a million years ago) I started keeping a diary, but after a week I just left it on the shelf to gather dust. Do real people keep diaries? I felt silly writing "Dear Diary" on the top of the page. Who was I talking to? Writing about my feelings made me nervous. The thought of it falling into the wrong hands was unsettling. My first week's entries dragged me down instead of lifting me up, so I abandoned the whole thing. However, it is possible to write down feelings and thoughts without feeling unnerved. You can nurture your emotions. I've kept a *"Baruch Hashem"* book for eight years (there are ten of them by now), and it has helped me look at life in new ways.

It's different than a diary or a journal. Unlike a diary, in a *Baruch Hashem* book you list the things you are thankful for instead of just aimlessly recording feelings. Since you write the good things happening to you, it is a positive experience. It also helps you capture those moments that would otherwise be long forgotten. Reading a page here and there can really help me calm down.

Take a few moments to savor your delightful memories.

You surely have successful moments every day. There are things that turn out better than you expected. The teacher loved your essay. You needed to make copies and you had the exact amount of money in your pocket. Your mother surprised you and brought home danishes for everyone. However, these pleasant moments tend to fade away while the problems tend to stand out. That's why it's important to save our positive experiences so we can relive them in the future.

Some people like to take pictures; I preserve the good moments by writing them down. Some people create scrapbooks or draw because they believe that a picture is worth a thousand words. Yet I like to write. We are all trying to capture something essential. By saving what is important to us we can create a more optimistic and pleasant atmosphere.

What should I write about?

Thank Hashem for the good things that happened to you and your siblings. Thank Hashem for good news that you heard about in your community. You can be happy that someone on the block got engaged, that your brother was on the honor roll and that your teacher decided not to give a quiz although she said yesterday that she would test you on thirty-five pages. You can feel grateful that you heard a bird singing, a child saying a *brachah*, the wind blowing in the trees, and your father's footsteps when he came home. Think of everyone who is healthy and safe. Think of a time that you fell and didn't hurt yourself. Rejoice in the gifts you received today.

Be happy that you were able to give. Did you put a quarter in the meter for someone or give a quarter to your friend who needed to make a phone call? I was about to board the bus and was short 15 cents for the fare. A 16-year-old boy was waiting for the same bus. He gave me the 15 cents. I promised to give the money to charity.

Afterwards, I gave $2 to charity, instead of just 15 cents. I felt so grateful that I was able to board that bus because someone I didn't know had been kind. Small gifts are significant.

There is a gift that many of you have given me. It's always a surprise and it always brightens my day. Sometimes a letter comes in the mail. A reader took the time to write and say, "I feel the same way. I understand. Thank you for writing this book." I appreciate your letters. Many of them are taped into my *Baruch Hashem* book.

A – Aspire
T – Take each day with you
T – Think up!
I – Identify with your ideals
T – Try to grow each day
U – Untie the bonds of anger and jealousy
D – Dream and hope
E – Every positive action brings you closer to Hashem

Do you think it's important to save your memories?

_____

_____

_____

How do you prefer to preserve your experiences?

_____

_____

_____

Do you take photos, draw, make a scrapbook, or do you write things down?

_____

_____

_____

Small Things

Should you wake
In dark of night
Say a few words.
It doesn't matter about what.

Say, "Thank you that
the baby's ear infection
went away."
Say, "Oh, help me please!
I'm so afraid of this new day."
Say, "Please give me strength. Please keep us all
alive and well."
Say, "May the Temple be rebuilt.
May Mashiach come today."
It doesn't matter what,
Just say a few words to G-d.
Don't think it's such a small thing.
What can it matter?
Of what importance can it be?
What harm if I don't?
What help if I do?
Because, first of all,
It's not a small thing.
It's a big thing.
And anyhow,
There are no small things.

Be Happy Now!
In This Moment Rejoice!

Thank You, Hashem

Gratitude is a mitzvah you can do in a minute. It's easy. It makes everything you do simpler and more enjoyable. Give form to your feelings by saying these three words, "Thank You, Hashem," and writing them down. Magnify your pleasant moments. There are no small things. Remember, thanking Hashem is a mitzvah.

The Rambam says that thanking Hashem is an essential part of prayer. There are two parts to prayer. When we pray we request and we contribute. During our prayers we ask Hashem for what we need. However, prayer is also supposed to be a present to Hashem. What are we giving when our main thought is our requirements? The Rambam tells us that when we say thank you to Hashem we fulfill the mitzvah of serving Hashem with our heart. When we give thanks, we convey to Hashem the admiration we owe Him (*Shaarei Tefillah*, R' Shimshon Pincus).

Celebrate that you feel well. Take a moment to notice that you had a good night's sleep. How many Torah tapes do you own? Thank Hashem for them. Did your friend knock on the door and surprise you? Thank Hashem for sending her. Did your cold go away? Acknowledge your health. If you remembered to count *Sefiras HaOmer*, it is not a small thing, so thank Hashem. Think about the great smell of challah baking and of fresh laundry. Think about a letter in the mail or something misplaced that was found. All of them are reasons to grab a mitzvah and thank Hashem. Don't wait for something big because there are no small things.

Each of us can access great feelings. This is true for everyone. We already have everything we need to connect with our better self. Listen to the whisper inside. However, if we don't know where to look we just continue floating through life day after day without taking advantage of the treasure that's inside us. As one famous author said, "It takes only a moment to change your attitude and in that moment you can change your day." Stop, smile, and thank!

THANK YOU, HASHEM, FOR

1. _____

2. _____

3. _____

4. _____

5. _____

❧ Have You Said "Thank You" to Hashem Today?

"*H*ave you said 'Thank You' to Hashem today?" These eight words changed my life. They have transformed difficult days and difficult jobs into happy ones full of gratitude. They helped me remember I could find something good in everything. Here are a few instances where I used these words to change my day.

My mother asked me to complete a chore for her. I was not in the mood to help at that moment. I wasn't! I wanted to relax. I was beginning to feel upset. I felt she asked me to help more than anyone else around here. Suddenly these eight words popped into my head. I began contemplating the idea. I said, "Thank you Hashem for giving me a mother to ask me to help her. There are many people who do not have one." In just a matter of minutes the job became easier.

On a wet, rainy day I was sitting indoors thinking about plans that had been interrupted by the weather. Did I have to feel gloomy? I was in charge. Instead of grumping about the dark, gloomy day and weather, I said, "Thank You, Hashem, for the rain. The cold drops can feel good on my cheeks. The rain makes everything grow." After saying these words I felt so good. I was happier than I had been before.

Words can change your life. These words have made my days easier. Thank You, Hashem, for empowering me with these wonderful words.

Nechoma P.

It Will Be Good

Enjoy the Present — It's a Gift

My young eyes grew misty. I looked at my scraped knee. It was bleeding! I wanted to be big. I didn't want to cry. My father came up from behind and helped me up. "It hurts but it will get better quickly," he said. "It will be good. By the time you are a bride you'll forget you ever fell."

I felt confused. I didn't want to feel optimistic now. I wanted to cry and brood over my knee. I kept looking at it to see if it was still bleeding. I limped even though I really didn't need to. "It will be better when I'm a bride. Oh! That seems a long way off. I want to feel better now."

Perhaps you have similar objections. "The idea you're describing sounds great — just put on rose-colored glasses," I hear you saying. "I know some people who are like that. However, when I try to look for the good, my mind is blank. It's a hard trait to develop if you weren't born like that. Most of the people I know don't smile too much. I'm always hearing the people around me complaining about one thing or another."

What does the ability to enjoy being alive depend upon? What circumstances hold people back from enjoying life? Could one take pleasure in life despite chronic pain? Is it possible to smile even when your car is out of order? How do you react when there is no hot water? What's your response when someone is late for an appointment? Winston Churchill said, "Never give up. Never. Never. Never."

Would you like to acquire some of that optimistic persistence? If you could look into the future and see that your problem will be resolved it will help you put your problems in perspective. However, right now you feel overwhelmed. How can you feel optimistic even when you are in the midst of a problem?

Stop everything and say these four words: **"It will be good!"**

Simple as these words may seem, the phrase "It will be good" is powerful. In fact, once stated it motivates and challenges you to be happy right now.

"It will be good" is an affirmation that you can always turn to when you are in need of a more balanced point of view. This is convincing positive thinking. It's a phrase that will unfailingly generate good results. It demands a switch to a better frequency in this moment.

That said, let's explore what is holding you back from enjoying life. We'll look into some of your reservations. Sometimes it takes more than just saying four words to really feel them. However, if you explore the idea and create your own personal, meaningful example of it, these same words become more helpful.

Does the pleasure you feel each day depend upon things outside of you that change every day, or does it depend on what's happening *within*? Let me tell you something—what really matters are the ideas inside of yourself. *If your joy depends on your attitude you can always be happy.* Now and forever, no one can take your contented feeling away. The Torah you learned will always be a part of you and it will help you have an optimistic outlook.

I encountered the power of an optimistic outlook when I spoke with my parents last week. My parents had just arrived in their apartment the previous night. Although thousands of people travel by plane each day, I always feel a bit nervous about it. I called to express my concern over how their flight had been and how they were managing. I knew that most probably everything was fine, but sometimes there are unexpected frustrations.

"Everything is wonderful," my father assured me. "The apartment looks lovely," my mother agreed. "The air is so pleasant. I can walk outside in November in shirtsleeves and enjoy the sunshine," my father added. "By the way," my mother commented, "the refrigerator is broken."

Visions of my struggles with old refrigerators in bungalow colonies flew into my mind. Just a few years ago I had to defrost the refrigerator every two weeks and I would blow-dry the ice to make it melt more quickly. My children would smile and say, "We're the only ones who have snow in the summer." I didn't remember laughing along.

"How are you coping?" I asked, alarmed.

I heard my mother's calm voice on the line. "Don't worry. We went out last night and bought ice and a dishpan and put it in the refrigerator. When I lived in Argentina in the 1950s, I had an ice box for two years. It'll be just fine with an ice box for a few days until the repairman comes."

"Mommy, that's the perfect answer to the problem!" I exclaimed. "Whenever people have trouble with the refrigerator they can just turn it into an ice box."

I remembered my neighbor whose fridge was broken this past summer. She had left her milk, juice and dairy products in our fridge. Running back and forth between the bungalows was a hassle. My neighbor had to buy new supplies every day. At one point my neighbor said, "If they don't fix the fridge today, I'd like to go home. This just doesn't feel like a vacation."

I felt so proud of my parents that I smiled as I spoke with them. My parents are my unsung heroes. Their quiet courage gives me a glowing optimistic feeling and helps me smile throughout the day. Of course, I call to give my parents pleasure and tell them how we all are coming along, but I am the one who gains the most.

It was Friday and the repairman had not come, yet my mother still sounded like her cheerful, unflustered self. "I met three of my friends in the elevator. I'm so happy they are here early. Don't worry about the refrigerator. I'm pretty sure the ice will keep things cold over Shabbos."

I can't start my day without a dose of my mother's optimism. Otherwise, I feel something is missing in my morning. My mother's words gave me a surge of energy. That's what a cheerful role model does for me.

I called again on Sunday morning. My father sounded triumphant. "The ice lasted longer than expected. It kept everything cold for 36 hours."

I will savor that moment. It was encouraging to hear my father's proud voice describing how he had responded to this challenge and found a solution. My parents were enjoying every hour of every day in so many ways. Their happiness wasn't dependent on appliances working as expected but on the ability to find the positive aspects in their daily life. Could I learn to enjoy the important things in life — health, family, nature, good food and peace, even when little things go wrong? The values you embrace at the start of your life will guide you in the future. My parents gave me a different perspective on those inevitable hassles that we all face so frequently.

About four days later the repairman came. My father's voice sang as he spoke, "It's cold now inside the refrigerator! Now things will be a little easier. I knew all along that everything would be good in the end. You know something, Roiza? My mother, *a"h,* used to say, 'My son always says that it will be good. He has extraordinary *bitachon*.' "

I will remember the counsel of my father, a man who built the community we know today. Out of the ashes he kept the Torah alive. Although he came to this country as a lone survivor he didn't give up. He learned a new language, new skills, raised a family and helped develop a community. He built a business relying only on his faith in Hashem and his resourcefulness. That same resourcefulness helps him every day. I hope I can learn this trait from him. "It will be good!"

The Gift
of a Great
Morning

The Gift of a Great Morning

Hashem, satisfy us in the morning with Your kindness and then we will sing out loud and rejoice throughout our days.
(Tehillim 90:14)

Every morning a person is like a new creation.

(Rav Shlomo Ganzfried/*Kitzur Shulchan Aruch)*

Good Morning

There is one crucial moment that you and I experience every single day. It may be at a different time each day but that moment suddenly arrives. If we think about it we will be ready for it and our entire day will be more productive. However most of us will experience this moment only with half of our senses and often hours will pass before we catch up. This moment is when we first wake up.

I know how hard mornings can be. I know how tempting it can be to press that snooze button. Yet I would like to recommend that you make time for your spirit instead of sleeping longer in the morning. A calm morning will help you have a much better day.

Would you give me $1 if I gave you $5 in exchange?

Start off right. Would you give me $1 if I gave you $5 in exchange? So give yourself 15 minutes in the morning and gain 12 productive hours in exchange. Your mood in the morning has a ripple effect. The beginning determines what the rest of the day will be like. The rest of your day — while running to catch a bus, hurrying to finish various errands, meeting important people — will reflect your morning's mood. It takes work to carve out a productive morning routine. You have to want to wake up early to have time for your *neshamah* even if it hurts to jump out of bed. If you let go and turn over, a half-hour will slip away before you realize you've overslept. Yet if you grab yourself at the first instant you won't be sorry. It is a very wise investment. You will benefit from the returns throughout the day. When R' Simcha Zissel of Kelm would wake up his young children in the morning, he would gently say to them, "Children, you are sleeping away when you have a kingdom to rule. The Almighty gave man dominion over the entire creation" (*Meoros HaGedolim*).

Are there early mornings that you've enjoyed? Perhaps remembering those magical mornings will motivate you to wake up early.

New York is not Eilat, but remembering that magical morning helps me have a different experience right here that is also enjoyable. My mind travels back eighteen years to that fall morning when I saw the sunrise over the desert in Eilat. At first the sky was inky black. In the middle of the desert there are no streetlights. All the stars had faded and there was no light shining at all. The mountains seemed gray. My friends were merely shadowy figures climbing the mountain ahead. The world was enveloped in mist. Was this real? The world appeared covered by a hazy blanket. It seemed that there was a moment of stillness when the universe was waiting with bated breath for a new day. Then the sun slowly rose over the Jordan River. The soldiers guarding us put down their guns and took out their *siddurim* and *tefillin*. We took out our *siddurim* as well. I didn't merely read the words of the prayer that morning; I felt them. I felt a tugging within to focus on each word. I was aware that a new world was waking up around me. Everything was coming alive and beginning anew.

This desert has never changed. Buildings, mail boxes, ski lifts, cars and roads do not obscure Hashem's Fingerprints. I can think about this sunrise on an ordinary morning and remember that every morning Hashem creates the world anew. I can pray like that again now, so many years later.

Take some time in the morning to enjoy who you are as you stand on the threshold of giving yourself the gift of today. Notice some tiny miracle of creation — a flower, a tree, even the seed of a fruit. What kind of day are you looking forward to? Remember that a great day often follows a great morning. How? You can only find out if you invest the time to wake up happy. One great way to begin your day is by focusing on your favorite morning memories.

Do you remember a morning that was special?
Can you write down some points under one of these topics?

1. You rushed to get up because it was your birthday or a different exceptional day.
2. You woke up early, but it wasn't because of a specific pressure, and you were able to spend some relaxed time doing something fun.
3. You finished something that you had worked on for a while early in the morning and spent the rest of the day feeling relaxed.
4. You took the time to eat a real breakfast together with the family.
5. Your watch stopped or your phone was off the hook and you had a quiet morning.
6. You knew that your favorite teacher would be starting your day off and her lesson really made your entire day better.

7. Your baby sister smiled and laughed and ran to you.
8. Someone told you an unexpected compliment and you smiled about it all day long.

Morning Walk

Some people look forward to vacation as a time to sleep late. I like to wake up early. When there are only five days why waste 15 hours sleeping late? My mother rises early and we walk together to the grocery. The sun is shining on the white pavement and the palm trees are waving in the breeze. This is a time for us to talk, connect and listen.

My mother has a wonderful quality that I strive to emulate. She knows how to put everything on hold and really enjoy time spent with her children and grandchildren. She can wash her hands, wipe them with a towel, and in an instant she is completely there for you. Nothing in the past or the future will intrude on the precious moments of this visit. Because my mother is really paying attention when we speak to her she often understands what we wanted to say even before we say it.

Morning Song

The harsh noises of the city usually drown out the soft music of Creation. Yet even in the city there is a time every day in the early morning when all the birds sing together. If you are up early enough you can hear it. It's an unbelievable sound to focus on when you open your eyes, and a great way to launch your day. Most days I sleep through this song and I wake up to screeching brakes or an alarm clock buzzing before I'm ready. Consequently, I have a knot in my stomach. However on those days that I hear all of creation singing to Hashem I feel calm and peaceful.

A Bird's Nest – the Wonder of It All

Sometimes it's not hard to get out of bed because there is something exciting you want to look at. For three glorious weeks we had a bird's nest on the windowsill right near my son's bed. We saw the birds building the nest out of twigs and leaves. My son thought the birds might be cold and offered them a corner of his blanket. The birds incorporated it into their nest. It was a tiny nest with two eggs in it. A brown father and mother dove took turns sitting on the eggs. Occasionally, we saw both birds hovering near the nest together. Every morning, as the children woke up, they would run over to see how the birds were faring. They were relieved to see that either the mother or father bird was still sitting on the eggs. It was a wonder of Hashem's creation and it was so close to us — just inches away.

Tuesday Mornings With Bonnie

By 8:50 Tuesday morning I'm hovering near the phone. At precisely 9 o'clock the telephone rings. It's Bonnie calling from Oregon. We are studying *Tehillim Treasury* by Rabbi Avraham Chaim Feuer. Can you imagine? I may feel that it's hard to pull everything together and be ready by 9 a.m., but for my partner it's 6 a.m. Yet Bonnie always sounds so cheerful and eager to learn something new that speaking with her puts a smile on my face for the day.

Mornings are a time of gratitude and hope. Often I wake up feeling so much better than I did when I went to sleep. David HaMelech tells us that in the morning we are more easily aware of the kindness of Hashem and we can tell it to others.

⤳⤳

Why is it so noisy in here? I share a room with only one sister. Who came in here so early in the morning? Why are there many voices shouting? I open my eyes and am astonished. It takes me a while to realize that my five best friends are in the room singing "Happy Birthday."

In an instant, I leapt out of bed, got dressed, posed for some pictures, and left my house. I was blindfolded with a soft gray scarf. We walked for what seemed like a year. I heard laughter around me. Finally I heard a door close. I knew I had reached my destination, but where was I? They sat me down and asked me what I wanted for breakfast. The scarf was removed. I realized I was in a dairy restaurant. I ordered my favorite breakfast.

After breakfast we walked to school in unison. Everyone laughed at my surprise and shock in the early morning. I felt euphoric. I wore a smile from ear to ear the entire day.

Mimi F.

৵৵

*W*hen I was in camp, sunrise was the most intriguing sight. On the last night of camp everyone got together and went to different spots on the camp grounds to see the sunrise. Some went to the lake, some to the basketball court and some to the field.

We sat around in groups of twenty or so girls and sang songs while someone played the guitar. We waited for the sun to rise. Each group sat with a feeling of togetherness that was as thick as the dew that was falling in the early morning haze.

As the sun rose in clouds of deep pinks and soft orange, you felt the beauty of all the Jewish souls sitting together watching one of Hashem's creations. The only thought that came to mind is how wonderful everything is that G-d has created. How lucky we are to be part of His chosen ones. G-d has given us a wondrous, beautiful world to enjoy.

Breindy S.

৵৵

*E*very morning is a special one. However, on some really wonderful mornings I spring out of bed with a bounce in my step and a joyous song on my lips.

On the morning of my brother's bar mitzvah I felt enthusiastic. It was the first bar mitzvah celebrated in our family. I felt my heart soaring high! I imagined how my parents must feel looking at my brother on his bar mitzvah day. The entire day was beautiful, but the feelings of the morning remain in my memory.

I experienced similar emotions on the morning after my little sister was born. With the sunlight streaming though my bed-

room window, I awoke. I felt an outburst of song and I thought my happiness had no bounds. I thanked Hashem for His unlimited kindness. We were blessed with a precious, healthy child. I was anxious to begin this day.

Likewise, I felt a sensational feeling the morning my sister got engaged. I woke up with a smile on my face stretching from ear to ear. I remember the intense feelings of gratitude I felt that morning. I couldn't stop thanking Hashem for helping my sister find her specific match among all the people in the whole wide world. The joy was intense and practically tangible. It was a great start to a great day.

Mornings like these are hard to capture in mere words. There are happy whispers from within that an extraordinary gift has been presented to you. A wonderful day is going to unfold soon.

Rivki K.

Glowing Moments

☙ *A Favorite Morning Memory –* *It's Just One Word*

Surprise

It wasn't what I had expected. I came in as the teacher and left as the student. I entered feeling confident and I left pondering a new path with hesitant steps. When I walked up the steps I was the experienced teacher who had taught many lessons, spoken for crowds numbering in the hundreds, and written thousands of words. I entered the room intending to speak. This encounter was different. The picture I perceived was different than anything I had seen before. I left as a student who had understood a familiar concept in a totally new way.

I entered through the white door with a large black bag that was filled with Torah books. Their weight on my shoulder gave me a sense of purpose. I had come on a mission. I crossed the threshold with a firm step. I didn't merely come to teach; I wanted my student to think. It wasn't enough to cover material, I hoped that something more would happen. I hoped my student would remember this morning encounter for a long time.

Why Had I Come Here?

I knew what had brought me to this particular kitchen. Something had made me hire a babysitter and come on a Sunday morning. It was her eyes. That intent gaze was filled with hunger and longing. I don't have words to describe the depth in those eyes. The seeking and the wisdom in her eyes grabbed me. It didn't let go either. Ten years later I remember her intent gaze. Her eyes looked directly at you during a conversation and gave you the feeling that your words mattered. I felt a little shy at this total attention to my words. I wondered, "Perhaps I possess a treasure that I wasn't aware of before."

She stood at the kitchen counter and greeted me calmly and happily as I entered. The room was filled with a delicious fragrance. The perfume she was wearing mingled with the scent of food cooking. "You've brought the food for the soul and I'm providing the food for the body." She was cutting scallions and grating carrots. A pot of brown liquid was simmering on the stove. "It's miso soup," she explained. "It cuts away at toxins and gives you energy." She reached into the fridge and extracted a spongy square, which she chopped into cubes. "This is tofu. It gives you protein and calcium. My sister says it tastes like any food you want to savor, like the manna the Jews ate in the desert." Her hands moved quickly and gracefully. She's a grandmother, but when she smiled she looked like a high-school student. Two beautiful bowls were filled with brown liquid.

Is This Breakfast?

I sat and stared at the bowl that was placed in front of me. I could not comprehend this. Is this breakfast? We sipped miso soup with brown rice and green seaweed instead of gulping cereal and milk. We refreshed ourselves with imitation coffee sweetened with molasses and whitened with soy milk instead of hot cocoa. In place of plastic the food was presented on heavy china plates with blue borders.

My silver soup spoon clinked in the bowl that had a picture of a Chinese house in the center. Wouldn't it be nice if I celebrated in this manner every Sunday? My friend repeated the recipe in case I wasn't concentrating, as I watched her cook: "Four cups of water, a tablespoon of miso, two grated carrots, three scallions, one-third of a block of tofu and a small piece of seaweed." She wants me to take home this knowledge. "You'll have more energy if you eat healthful foods."

Glowing Moments

What was happening? Hadn't I come to do the teaching today? In just a few moments I felt that I was the student. As we proceeded to open the Torah book I realized that this might be a very memorable teaching moment. There are special moments when you not only teach but also reach your student. You explain something and as you think it over together you touch something just for a moment. You grasp a concept that's above you. It's like a flash of lightning. You feel that this is eternity. This really matters. It's so hard to get a moment like this down on paper. The words all sound the same.

Insight is something one notices. One hears that deep breath or that long sigh. The eyes sparkle with understanding. The person's face glows and their eyes sparkle. Their head nods, acknowledging a flash of wisdom. Words cannot adequately capture that moment.

The Merit of One Word

The sun was streaming in through the large sliding glass doors. I took out the Torah books and began the lesson. We learned that in the merit of answering one word — *Amen* — when a blessing is said, G-d saved the Jews from their enemies during the period of Deborah the Prophetess.

We read about the incident in the Prophets. We read through Deborah's song of praise after the Jews were miraculously saved. Siserah had attacked with an alliance of twenty-one kings and an army that was as numerous as the sand on the shore. Yet a small Jewish army triumphed. Deborah sang, "G-d defeated our enemies because the Jews blessed G-d."

Then I read from a pocket-size volume of the Talmud: "This miracle occurred in the merit of the word *Amen*. In the merit of *Amen* evil decrees are erased. Whoever says *Amen* with all his powers of concentration will have the gates of the Garden of Eden opened for him." I looked at my student over our china bowls and said, "Hashem is listening. Every word counts. Every letter is measured."

We thought it over quietly. It was a concept that can transform one's life. One word is that powerful. Answering *Amen* can provide protection against those who are trying to destroy us. Answering *Amen* can help you enter the Garden of Eden.

"It's just one word!" I exclaimed.

My student smiled and then she made a comment. Her few words contained a lesson that I'll always remember.

"It's just one word," she repeated, "but there's a catch."

"What?" I asked.

"It has to be with heart."

"It has to be with sincerity and heart," I repeated. Think when you speak. Think about why you are saying *Amen*. Ponder what it is that you firmly believe. Remember Who is listening to that one word, *Amen*. Every time, every day, when we say *Amen* we can decide. Will that moment be average or extraordinary?

Insight!

The instant you realize that we are all a part of something truly great feels better than delight. You feel that every moment of your ordinary life connects with an eternal heavenly dimension. Something we have done hundreds of times can have a superior effect. It's a choice we really do have.

Will that moment be average or extraordinary?

Begin Your Day With a Song and a Smile

The kind of life you'll live forever depends on what you do TODAY.

(R' Ezriel Tauber)

•◦ *What a Wonderful Morning*

"What a wonderful morning.
I will start it with a song.
I will say my Modeh Ani
Would you like to sing along?
All we have to say is thank you
I'm so glad that I woke up
It's another wonderful morning
And I'll start it with a song."

I remember singing this jingle at lineup in day camp. When I was younger it was just a song. However, as I grow older I realize more and more how true this is.

It really is appropriate to begin each day with a song, a smile, and a feeling of gratitude. Every day is a gift from the Almighty. It is a chance to accomplish and grow. We have to be thankful when we get up every morning alive and well. There are mornings when I get up and pull aside the mini-blinds and simply stare. The birds are chirping. The trees are swaying. The sun is shining. Everything is calm and peaceful. I sit there and think to myself, "How awesome are Hashem's creations."

I spent this summer with my wonderful grandmother. She likes to go to bed early in order to wake up early and enjoy the calm and serene summer morning. Every day she enthusiastically described the beauty of the country in the early morning. Morning is a wonderful time to thank Hashem for His beautiful creations.

My grandmother knows how to encourage. Her gentle words make me smile. She might say, "Look how smart you look today." When I mutter, "Oh, it's just a simple blouse and skirt," she'll reply,

"True, but your blouse is a lovely shade of blue and it's so crisp and clean I can see the pleat on the sleeve." After I call a friend she might comment, "You're so thoughtful. You have a knack for finding the right words." Mornings remind me of my grandmother.

Next time your alarm clock rings, don't mumble. Instead, wake up with a song, a smile, and a feeling of gratitude. Enjoy the wonderful morning.

Rochel Esther N.

⁓ᲜᲜ⁓

For many of us, a visit with someone we admire awakens or intensifies our ability to enjoy life. We find new dimensions inside us, new interests in our everyday lives. Small things that we encounter daily remind us of that special person. Lofty ideals become more accessible. The first hour of the brand new day we too are brand new. It's a wonderful time to think about the people we admire.

What's your favorite morning memory?

_____

_____

_____

❧ *There Are No Ordinary Days*

Hashem does miracles for us all the time. He hopes that we will realize this and thank Him. We are healthy and alive today. Have we sincerely thanked Hashem? Do we pray with proper concentration or do we just mumble the words? If our words are not clear are our prayers valid?

I thought about these ideas when I encountered death for the first time. I was completely shocked when my grandfather passed away. I realized that we are here for only a short time and we should not take that time for granted. I never realized that having a grandfather is a gift. I should have cherished every moment with him because now I can't be with him.

Do we praise Hashem enough? Since I lost my grandfather I try to concentrate more on the prayers. I'm careful to pronounce each word clearly. Hashem does what no one else can.

It's important to love every minute of life. It is normal to love life when you are a lottery winner or be disappointed with life when you hear bad news. However, we should love life even when we've had a boring day. Every ordinary day is a miracle.

Raizy S.

∽◌∾

❧ When the Morning Sky Turned Gray

September 11, 2001 began in an ordinary way. I woke up early, complained that school should start an hour later, and packed my lunch. I was surprised that my father was still at home. He was searching for his misplaced glasses. After 20 minutes of searching he found them in his suit pocket. He left late for his job in Manhattan. A short time later I left for school.

After Shacharis at 10:30 my classmates were all busy reviewing for our next class. The noise level had reached a high. A teacher walked in and suggested that we stop everything and say Tehillim. She explained that the Pentagon had been hit and the World Trade Center was destroyed. The class sat there shocked. Suddenly fear gripped my heart.

Was my family safe? Outside the sky darkened with ash and the air smelled like death. I sat in my seat saying Tehillim. The words blurred because of my tears. The same thoughts whirled in my head over and over — my father, my brother, my father, my brother. I can't describe the dread I felt.

My married brother had woken up early to go to Selichos. His boss had requested that he come in early to his job in the city. When he returned from the synagogue, the baby was crying and *throwing up. At 8:50 a.m., while still at home, he heard that a plane had crashed into one of the Twin Towers. He thought, "That's not my building," and left for work.*

There was nothing unusual about his subway ride. The familiar stops passed, one by one. He rode through the dark tunnel and over the bridge. My brother would later wonder how everything in the subway car had remained the same. Everyone was calm.

Around 9:30 he walked up the steps of the subway station and looked toward his office at World Financial Center. He saw a horrifying sight — people were jumping off the World Trade Center! Then the rumbling started and the dust made breathing and seeing nearly impossible. As the building began to collapse, he turned and ran for his life.

Meanwhile I was back in school, frantically trying to call home. When I finally got through, my brother's first words were, "Everyone is accounted for." I felt relieved. It was as if a stone was lifted off my chest. I realized in that instant that life is precious and family means more than anything else. When I returned home I gave everyone an extra long hug, thankful that they were safe.

We stand at the crossroads of life. We don't know where the roads will lead and whether they will be full of bumps or smooth for miles. No matter what happens we should be thankful for the precious gifts with which G-d has endowed us. No day is ordinary.

Miriam Brocho Minzer

The Gift
of Health

❧ *Seeing – for the First Time*

by Helen Keller

She brought me my hat, and I knew I was going out into the warm sunshine. This thought, if a wordless sensation may be called a thought, made me hop and skip with pleasure.

We walked down the path to the well-house, attracted by the fragrance of the honeysuckle with which it was covered. Someone was drawing water and my teacher placed my hand under the spout. As the cool stream gushed over my hand she spelled into the other hand the word water, first slowly, then rapidly. I stood still, my whole attention fixed upon the motion of her fingers. Suddenly I felt a misty consciousness as of something forgotten — a thrill of returning thought; and somehow the mystery of language was revealed to me. I knew then that W-A-T-E-R meant the wonderful cool something that was flowing over my hand. That living word awakened my soul, gave it light, hope, joy, set it free!

As we returned into the house, every object I touched seemed to quiver with life. That was because I saw everything with the strange, new sight that had come to me.

Think about your ability to see. List ten things you are able to do with the gift of vision. Your world is full of pleasures that vision gives you, such as: seeing your family's and friends' faces, watching a sunset, admiring a bouquet of flowers, and choosing your outfit every morning. A distant cousin who was a widower seemed to see things just as well as I did. However, whenever we met at family celebrations his clothes didn't match. His jacket might be blue and his pants black while his tie contained shades of brown. We were all thrilled when he remarried. One day I met this cousin and complimented him, "Your suit looks nice and that tie goes well with it."

"Actually, I'm color blind," he admitted. "Now that I'm married my wife chooses my outfits and hangs everything I need for that day on one hanger."

This cousin made me look more closely at the gift of seeing color. I asked myself, "How would I cope without this gift?" Would I be able to do needlepoint, take photos, decorate scrapbooks or shop for my own clothes? Suddenly all those things became more precious to me than they had been before.

So make that list now from one to ten. Let your imagination flow. Once you finish your list sit back and savor each item you wrote down. You can make your life more enjoyable in just a few moments. It's no more difficult to make this list than it is to complain and grumble because something you hoped for didn't happen.

1. _____

2. _____

3. _____

4. _____

5. _____

6. _____

7. _____

8. _____

9. _____

10. _____

～∂∽

Of course Esty said the same blessing as the rest of us, thanking Hashem for the gift of sight. However, Esty never thought about her eyes until one particular summer afternoon. It happened in just one minute. One minute you are coasting along totally involved in the game of life, in the middle of the competition, focused on accomplishing, running to the goal. A moment later you are someone in pain, alone, trying to stay afloat, worried and vulnerable.

This past summer, I was having a great time playing outfield during a baseball game. A player hit an easy fly ball near me. I quickly raced backwards and stuck out my glove to catch the ball. Instead of landing in my mitt, the ball fell with a bang into my right eye. Everything turned black and I fell to the ground.

Several hours later, I was finally allowed to leave the infirmary. I was in terrible pain, but it was worse than that. I couldn't see because of the tremendous swelling. While walking around without being able to see out of one eye, I began appreciating all the days when I could see normally. This experience taught me to say my prayers with more concentration. I say 'thank You' to Hashem not only for extra gifts but also for the gifts that many of us take for granted.

Esty O.

Esty felt a sense of overwhelming gratitude. Before the accident, she had never realized just how much she possessed. Close your eyes for a moment and try to "see" the first thing your hand can reach just by feeling it. Now open your eyes. Do you see it differently than before? Your optimistic thoughts can serve you well in any situation. Focusing on the simple things you can do provides you with spiritual armor. You view life from a healthier perspective.

Make the two words *"Baruch Hashem"* part of your everyday vocabulary, and help the gratitude revolution grow. When you hear that someone had a baby, say *"Baruch Hashem."* Perhaps add the prayer, "May we always celebrate." Feel joyous, because as the anecdotes below point out, every healthy baby is a miracle.

∽◌∾

Mrs. Bell's infant was born six and a half weeks early. Baruch Hashem everything went smoothly. It was better than the doctors had expected. However, her little bundle of joy was born with underdeveloped lungs. The situation was rather serious. She says that it is such a miracle that he's fine today because there were so many aspects that could have gone wrong but Baruch Hashem didn't. It's truly incredible how fast he progressed. The doctors predicted that her infant would be released from the hospital around his due date. Two hopeful days later, he was suddenly breathing like any newborn. It was a real miracle! One week later he had his bris.

Even after the danger had passed there were so many other things that could have gone wrong. Baruch Hashem, they didn't. At about age 2, he was up to par with other children his age, although he was small.

We have to be thankful to Hashem for the miracles He does every day. We don't have to search very far. We should not only appreciate the big miracles but also the seemingly small things. We can't take anything for granted.

Tzeena W.

∽◌∾

Sometimes I volunteer to help handicapped children. The feelings of gratitude I have when I pray on those days are inspired by the realization that I have more than others.

How many times have I complained while walking somewhere that it's such a long walk and I wish I could go by car? Then I stop and think — what about those who can't walk?

Simi S.

✦

When you answer the telephone and someone asks how you are feeling, don't just mumble, "I'm okay." Say instead, "*Baruch Hashem* I'm feeling excellent." Send a birthday card or a letter to congratulate a new mother. It's a wonderful way to remember that every child is a miracle. Find ways to say *Baruch Hashem* every day and remind others what a delight life is.

What's Inside the Box?

I'm sitting in front of my computer and thinking back to my graduation. I remember sitting in a blue robe and graduation cap in one of the three front rows on the right and listening to the speeches. The cameras flashed as each speaker rose to say something momentous. Each speaker illustrated his point with a different story. I don't remember their words but I do remember the stories.

After the speeches our principal and assistant principal called out each name in alphabetical order and handed out diplomas and yearbooks. Patiently we waited until each girl was called. The silence was interrupted only by applause as each graduate paused for a moment, said thank you as she received her diploma and slowly walked along the stage and down the steps again. Finally the last graduate, S. Zabare, received her diploma. Then the music began once again. This time we marched out to a lively tune.

I look out the window and see the sun shining on the tree in my backyard. I see a small patch of blue sky. I think about the stories I heard at my graduation and I realize that those stories are still important. As I look around, I see those stories in a different way.

I've collected many stories since graduation. Every day I increase my treasury of stories and learn more insights. There are times when a simple story goes straight to your heart. The ideas in the story mean so much more than the story itself. The metaphor in a story can be applied to many situations. This is a story about a unique gift that has lasting value. Reminding yourself about it is invaluable and energizing when you feel you can't go another inch. By remembering it you will realize how great is this one word of just four letters.

A gift can be a treasure. Sometimes a gift comes in a beautifully wrapped box, but what really counts is what's inside. The size of the box does not necessarily tell us much about the value of a gift. Sometimes something really valuable comes in a small package. It's important to appreciate a gift. Two people may receive an identical gift. One person will cherish it while the other one will find fault.

I met my friend one day. She looked forlorn and depressed. I asked her what was the matter. She said that she felt neglected and hurt. Her parents and her relatives seemed to shower all their attention upon her sister who wasn't feeling well. "My sister receives many presents," she complained.

I tried to convince her that she had the better part of the deal — she was healthy. However, she simply shrugged her shoulders.

How could I help this friend? I walked into a store and purchased gift-wrap. I took a small box and wrapped it with the colorful gift-wrap. I placed it inside a larger box, also gift-wrapped, then put that in a larger box, and so on. I added bows and stickers and other decorations.

When I handed the gift to my friend her eyes twinkled. She felt content because someone had thoughtfully given her a gift. She opened up one layer of gift-wrap and then another. Finally she was down to the last wrapper. Inside was a tiny box. She opened it and found a piece of elegant parchment paper. There were only four letters on that piece of paper written in large calligraphy script. My friend read it and nodded. She smiled and hugged me tightly.

Those four letters spelled L-I-F-E !

The greatest gift we can receive is the gift of life. After a gift is used its value usually decreases. Life is a different sort of gift. The more you use it the greater its value. It is a gift that increases in value with each passing day.

Rivky F.

❧

Are you beginning to get the idea of how to enjoy every ordinary day? Ordinary blessings are hidden from us until we take the time to notice them. Have some of these examples helped you to discover a new perspective? Here's hoping you'll add some ideas of your own.

I thought about this and I believe I found a good way to look at your day from the very start:

Close your eyes for a second and imagine that when you awake in the morning someone hands you a huge box. The box is covered with gold foil wrap and adorned with six colorful ribbons. You sit up and think to yourself — there must be something really good in this beautiful box. Well, there is — it is the gift of L-I-F-E, and it is yours each day.

Trading Treasures

The next time you meet with your best friend, change an ordinary cardboard box into a treasure box. You may want to decorate it with gift-wrap and ribbon. Now the fun can begin. Take turns filling the box with meaningful treasures and then leave it for each other to find. Everyone has days when they could use a surprise. Perhaps your friend is going to a job interview for camp. Wouldn't she love to find a surprise in her locker with an encouraging note and a treat on that day? The box then becomes her obligation. Now it is her turn to prepare a surprise for you. Every time you exchange the box mark the date inside the box's lid. See how long you can continue exchanging the treasure box. There are two friends who did this for five years. Wow!

The Gift
of Prayer

Be careful what you pray for — you just might get it.

(Rav Mendel Kaplan)

Imagine someone finds and picks up a wallet filled with money while walking down the street, but he doesn't smile or jump for joy. You would conclude that he doesn't understand what money is worth. If we pray and we aren't happy that we can pray, then do we understand what prayer is worth?

(Rav Shimshon Pincus)

Today I am going to really make time to pray. Prayer helps me find joy and greatness in a special way.

A Prayer Chart —
Do You Know Your ABC's

A- Always Pray! This is an absolute must. There are so many reasons not to pray today: I don't have time. I can't concentrate. I will open the *siddur* anyhow, because if I skip a day it will be harder to pray tomorrow.

B- Begin: When I begin my day with prayer it's so much better. If I wake up early and talk to Hashem before I talk to anyone else it is so much easier to focus and to pray from my heart.

C- Clear: I make each word count when I say it clearly.

D- Don't delay! I know it's wrong. So many times I tell myself I'll just do one thing first. Suddenly it's 11:30.

E- Enthusiasm: Rav Shimshon Pincus said that we should be happy that we can pray and appreciate its value. Imagine your joy at finding a sum of money and pray with at least that much joy.

F- Focus on one part: If I can't concentrate on *all* of the prayers, I should begin with one sentence, then one paragraph, etc.

G- Gratitude to Hashem: Expressing gratitude is one of the reasons I was created. I want to remember when I say a blessing that I am now saying thank you!

H- Hope: I think of the times that I was worried or afraid and Hashem answered me. I hope that Hashem will answer me now.

I- Insight: Every day try to learn something about the prayers and gain a new insight.

J- Jerusalem: We all face Jerusalem when we pray. I should concentrate and pray with conviction, "Hashem, return to Your holy city with compassion!"

K- Kindness: My prayer is an act of kindness when I pray for someone else.

L- Love Hashem: Every time you stop and say, "I love You, Hashem!" it's a mitzvah.

M- Mistakes: When I realize that I made a mistake and my mind wandered, I don't waste a moment. I start to focus immediately!

N- New: Today I am a new person. Today Hashem created a new world. Today is a new beginning.

O- One: Hashem is one. Hashem is the one and only in the seven heavens and the four corners of the earth. When I say the last word of *Shema* (*echad*) I pause to focus on this thought.

P- Plan: I want to plan before I pray. Right now what am I trying to say to Hashem?

Q- Quiet: Quiet time is necessary for a prayerful mind.

R- Reconsider: Have another look at the prayer you just said.

S- Sincerity: I remember that every time I pray I am talking to the Master of the Universe, and I must do so with conviction.

T- Time: I must try to use my prayer time in the best way possible.

U- Unexpected: Unexpected miracles happen every day.

V- Victory! Rabbi Feuer explains that Hashem wants to grant us victory. Hashem wants us to overturn difficult decrees through our prayers.

W- Wisdom: Wisdom is using what I learned to help me pray in a better way.

X- X-pect: Expect Hashem to always help.

Y- Yet: If my prayer was not answered I won't give up. It may not be answered yet but I still continue to hope and pray.

Z- Zeal: I will try to pray with fervor and bring my prayers to the zenith.

*M*y teacher shared a beautiful and inspiring idea with us, one that she herself had implemented. She went to a Judaica store and purchased two identical wooden bentcher holders. Upon arriving home she hammered the two bentcher holders into the kitchen wall so that they were side by side. She placed an entire set of Tehillim booklets into one of the holders. When her children arrived home she gathered them around the table and motioned for silence. She pointed to the wooden holders on the wall and said, "Children, while you wait for your egg to boil or for your bread to toast, instead of looking at your watch and willing those moments away, take a booklet from that box and use it. While you are waiting for your friend to come to the phone, instead of staring idly out the window take a booklet and recite those precious words. When you are done simply put it into the adjoining holder so by the time the day draws to an* *end the once-empty compartment will now be filled with words of prayer that were said."*

Once a moment passes it is lost, swept away with the sands of time, but the moments of reciting Tehillim will be yours eternally.

Zissy W.

Many of us sway in prayer. Rabbi Schwab explains that the swaying expresses dual emotions — a longing to cling to Hashem and, a moment later, an unconscious pulling back in awe.

Prayer

Do you remember the times in your life when prayer was an intense experience? I recall the time I stood near the wall in fourth grade and prayed so intensely that the class went down to the assembly and I still wasn't finished. There was the time that I discovered the *Hirsch Siddur* in ninth grade, after my grandmother had passed away, and I began to realize the magnificent meaning of the words we say. I remember an intense longing to cleave to Hashem and a simultaneous fear and pulling back.

I visualize the Tomb of Rachel and wonder if she is crying for her children. When I saw the crowds by her tomb all praying intensely it made me feel as if it were Yom Kippur. On Yom Kippur we stand spiritually on tiptoe and pray from deep inside. Once, when I was 8, I was playing outside on Yom Kippur and when I rushed in to shul I saw my mother praying and crying. I asked her later why she had cried and she said, "I cried to Hashem to always be with you and help you."

It is possible to be surrounded by waves of prayer. You can experience this in shul on Shabbos or Yom Tov. Every week, when our *Tehillim* group gathers, each person takes a booklet and together we finish the entire Psalms. A feeling of sanctity surrounds us as we fervently recite the timeless words of David Hamelech.

Life's greatest challenge is converting our ideals into reality.

We know that when we open up our prayerbook and say the words, we are speaking to the Master of the Universe. We have heard many stories about the power of prayer. Our teachers have told us the importance of praying with our souls. They have also told us that our humble words can create a ripple effect throughout the cosmos. Yet are we truly aware when we pray? Do we really see prayer as a conversation with Hashem?

How can one be aware of holiness?

Rabbi Weinberg explains this difficult concept with an image. Imagine that you meet a friend sitting in a room with a blindfold covering her eyes. She is also wearing headphones, and noise is flooding her ears from a Walkman. As you enter you realize that there is a joyous wedding celebration taking place in that room, but your friend with the blindfold and the headphones complains, "I don't see anything. I don't hear anything." It's obvious to you that your friend can only see and hear if she opens her eyes and ears. Likewise, there is a sixth sense, a spiritual sense in our hearts, that we must access in order to be aware of holiness.

If we pray with an open heart we will look forward to prayer. Prayer is a conversation. We are speaking with the King of the universe. When we speak to Hashem and approach Him as our father, then we become princesses. We discover our royalty.

An Audience With the Queen

The first time I visited London, I was 6 years old. My mother held my hand as I stood on the sidewalk near a throng of people. We watched hundreds of soldiers clad in red coats marching precisely back and forth.

"Who lives inside the big palace?"

"This is Buckingham Palace, and the Queen of England lives inside. These are her guards," Mother explained.

"Will we be visiting her today?"

"Not today," my mother laughed. "One must make an appointment to see the queen months in advance. Only distinguished people are given the opportunity to see her. She doesn't visit with ordinary people."

About fifteen years later I visited London again. Our family took a summer trip to Israel and we stopped over in London on the way home. I said, "I want to go to London. I don't need to go sightseeing. I don't have to visit the palaces or the Tower of London or shop at Harrod's. I want to visit Mrs. Schlaff. I want to see this unique friend of the family again." I'm glad I went, because this was my last visit with her.

I walked up the cobblestone path and knocked on the door of 40 Lewiston Place. To reach this address, I had not come from around the corner; I had traveled across an ocean. Her grandchild was leaving the house and he held the door open for me. Why had I traveled such a long distance for this visit?

I walked past the dining room and noticed that a majestic Shabbos table was already set for the midday meal. Every detail was perfect. The elegant china, silver place settings, and real cloth napkins all lent an aura of celebration. Indeed, the Shabbos Queen was in this home. Several red roses stood guard in a crystal vase.

I arrived at a small room off the kitchen. I stood in the doorway. Mrs. Schlaff was sitting, reciting *Tehillim*. What should I do? I didn't want to disturb her, so I stood and watched. Now, many years later, I still feel elated when I recall the moment.

In front of Mrs. Schlaff was a big leather-bound book of *Tehillim*. I could hear her softly whisper words that in all likelihood were heard throughout the firmament. I felt a spark because Mrs. Schlaff was smiling. Few people smile when they say *Tehillim*. There was confidence and serenity in the air. Perhaps it's difficult for us to say *Tehillim* with a smile because we feel a nagging doubt in our hearts. Is Hashem really listening to our humble words? Yet her words were clearly being said to Someone. She was saying each word with total concentration. She realized how great each simple word of *Tehillim* really is and that gave her strength. After a sentence she would pause and close her eyes. It was clear that she was thinking and listening, not just saying words by rote. This prayer was a dialogue with Hashem. As she said *Tehillim* her face lit up with perception. She grasped prayer in a way that I couldn't fathom.

I sighed. How often do I barely hear what I am saying when I pray? How often do I just want to finish? Have I ever experienced *Tehillim* in this profound way? Is it possible for the words of *Tehillim* to speak to me? Can one feel the comfort of the Almighty's closeness? Can the Shabbos Queen dwell in my modest home? Can this faith and acceptance be attained on a daily basis or on an ordinary Shabbos morning?

Ten minutes had passed. My hostess still had not noticed me and I didn't want to disturb her. Then I realized what I could do. I saw a *Tehillim* on the shelf. Quietly I reached for the prayer book and opened it. Softly, I sat down nearby with my *Tehillim* and joined Mrs. Schlaff. I felt that my prayers were ascending on the wings of hers.

For a long while Mrs. Schlaff didn't say a word. She simply looked directly into my eyes and smiled.

I had crossed the ocean to say *Tehillim*. I remembered the imposing palace I had seen in London years ago. Where was royalty? Now I knew that it was in a small kitchen at 40 Lewiston Place. This was the real royal residence. I had finally had an audience with the queen.

I'm Not Alone

There comes a time when you need to reach out and ask for help. Sometimes you can gain strength from the people you know. You can turn to people who see things as you do or perhaps can offer a different perspective. Sometimes you can find someone who has similar interests and you can develop a mutually beneficial relationship. It's fine to ask for help in addition to offering assistance. A group of friends can help one another. In school we learn not only from our teachers but from our fellow students. Every person has unique wisdom. It's not found in books. It's found in life.

However, there will also be times when our friends or family cannot help us. Something may be happening to you that no other human being can understand. Whom do you turn to when this happens and you feel alone?

Whom do you turn to with the difficult problems? Is there a solution when a problem seems overwhelming? I think you know the answer already. Perhaps you've worked out this procedure for yourself, through your own efforts. It's an answer that is simple yet difficult at the same time. You surely have heard this advice in class or read about it before. However, sometimes a simple anecdote can give you a new perspective. An anecdote shows you how someone else deals with problems. This can be more helpful than simple instructions. Whom do you turn to when you feel alone?

When I feel overwhelmed I turn to Hashem for support. I remember one day when there were so many things to take care of and then I had to deal with an emergency. I felt overwhelmed and worried. I began running around aimlessly. Finally I said, "Master of the Universe, I can't worry anymore! I can't deal with all of this. I'm giving it over to You." I felt so unburdened afterwards. It was excellent. Now I don't even remember what the emergency was. Hashem took care of it for me

a workshop participant

Prayer is a magical force. In my experience there is no other area of personal growth where one who is earnest can make such enormous strides in so short a time. However, there are three difficulties that turn up when we pray and try to really connect with Hashem.

First, it is difficult to have a conversation with our Creator. It is possible to pray and still feel alone. It's hard to visualize that we are talking to our Father and King, the Creator. We may have prayed since we were 3 years old and began saying *Modeh Ani* in the morning. Although the words flow easily, it's hard to truly say them with heart. To conclude that if we cannot concentrate properly we should just give up is absurd. There are a dozen ways to overcome this difficulty. Patient effort in this area is very worthwhile.

Second, there are individuals who have experienced real prayer but can't seem to repeat the experience. There is an obvious explanation: Perhaps it happened at a special place such as the Western Wall in Jerusalem, or it was at a special time such as Yom Kippur, or it was while standing near someone inspiring. At first glance the person may think that he has to be in the same place or near the same person to have this experience again, but that isn't so. The spark hidden inside can be kindled again.

The third difficulty is that it takes time to pray. It requires time alone, away from the routine and its distractions. One needs to say the words slowly and think about what they mean. Perhaps the phone begins ringing just when the heart is stirring. Don't despair — time can be made.

I learned a lot about prayer in school; however, the learning did not stop then. I search in books to find deeper meaning in the words of the *siddur*. I listen to tapes about prayer. The best lesson about prayer was the one I learned from a 7-year-old girl whom I never met.

Every year when it's *Parashas Chayei Sarah*, I think of this special child. Every year, I remember a casual conversation with Brocha Yafit's mother that initiated five years of weekly Shabbos lectures. I recall the story that pushed Shoshana, her mother, to host the lectures and convinced me to give them.

⚮

"We began to realize something was terribly wrong when Brocha Yafit was about 5 years old. We traveled hundreds of miles and saw the best doctors in the best hospitals. There were hundreds of needles and X-rays, procedures and blood tests. The operations followed. By the time Brocha Yafit was 7, she had endured more pain than many adults experience in their entire lives. Yet, every day, Brocha Yafit woke up and smiled. When she said Modeh Ani, one felt that she was talking directly to Hashem.*

It was late at night and Brocha Yafit lay near me in the hospital bed. She had no hair because of the chemotherapy. Her face looked pale and her eyes were dark with a deep sadness. I told her, "Please try to get some sleep."

"I can't sleep!" Brocha Yafit said. "After the surgery I felt better, but now it hurts here and here and in so many places."

My heart, my mother's heart, was full of anguish. I had changed my views about what was really important. I knew that I had to make the most of each hour and each day. I couldn't make plans. I tried to be brave. Brocha Yafit expected it. Yet, at this moment, I just froze. "Borei Olam, why? She is so frail and weak. Why must my child suffer? Why must she be in pain? I can't continue. I can't bear her pain. Borei Olam, help me!"

Brocha Yafit smiled bravely. "Mother, you can go to sleep. I can see that you are very tired. You need to rest. Don't worry about me. Surely you can see that Hashem is right here with me. The Borei Olam gives me strength and comforts me. I'll be fine while you rest. Go to sleep. I won't be alone. Hashem is right here with me."

❧

This little girl whom I never met gave me the inner strength to say, "Yes, if you decide to open your house and host the *Parashah* class I'll speak each week on Shabbos." Those lectures were satisfying. I looked forward to meeting my neighbors and doing something that would really make a difference.

It wasn't easy every week. There was the time I couldn't find someone to babysit and Shoshana sent her sons to watch my four children. Often I'd be frantically reading books on the *Parashah* right after lighting candles, because I still didn't know what I'd speak about in two hours' time. However, we always had the class and we never missed a week.

I know that Brocha Yafit's story is sad, but that's not what I felt when I first heard it and that's not what I remember when I think of Brocha Yafit. There are so many moments when I wonder what to do next. Whenever I need a helping hand I remember that I'm not alone. I just remember those courageous words spoken by a 7-year-old girl: "I'm not alone; Hashem is right here with me."

You never can know ahead of time when the opportunity will present itself for you to do something great. Perhaps if you always ask yourself, "How can I make the most of my day?" you will rise to the occasion when you have the chance. When the time comes, just two things matter — first, can you actually do what is required based on what you've heard and learned and seen? Second, do you have the courage to act and actualize your convictions? Don't be afraid of high expectations. Just begin and when you look back you will realize that you have traveled a road you never could have envisioned.

Connections

How many times have you made a promise to yourself to change? Yet weeks later everything is the same. You know what's right but acting on that knowledge is an entirely different story. For example, you know not to talk *lashon hara,* you know not to get angry, and you know that prayer is important. Why don't you pay attention and connect with the little voice inside you? Why don't you listen? Perhaps because it's so little that you can just pretend you didn't hear it. It's hard to change, even if you know that it's important.

A new place can help you make a new start. A new place can help you see something you've done many times in a new way. Serenity and freedom may envelop you. You can dip into a reservoir you were not aware of before. It feels good to be free.

This week I woke up at 6 a.m. and decided to pray with the sunrise. I walked into a new shul. I had no connections to this place. There were only two other insomniacs in the women's section and I had never met them before. I chose a seat in the back corner. I took a *siddur* and a *Chumash* from the shelf and put them before me. I opened the *siddur* and listened for the voice of the *chazzan* on the other side of the *mechitzah.*

I didn't care if I swayed. I didn't care if I cried into my *siddur.* I was free to be me. I was free from curious eyes and disapproving glances. I didn't have to hide. I didn't have to apologize for praying with my entire being. The nagging voice that had previously stopped me as I tried to soar in prayer was silenced. There were no interruptions.

I didn't turn when the door opened because I knew that I didn't know the woman entering anyway. For two hours I didn't talk to anyone. No one came up to me, so I didn't have to listen to someone chatter in order to be polite. I just listened to the *Parashah* and prayed. If there was a spare moment I said *Tehillim*. For two hours, I soared on the wings of prayer. I took as long as I needed to say each word.

I have heard for years that one should not talk in shul, but I always made exceptions. This woman will be insulted. Another one will look at me with a raised eyebrow, "What happened to you? Suddenly I'm not good enough for you. Why did you stop talking?" Yet I had learned that Hashem comes to join us in our house of prayer, but when we talk we push His presence away from our midst. This week I was relieved of the responsibility of compromising on an important value to make people comfortable with me. I felt so peaceful. I felt so calm within.

I realized that when we go to shul we really should try to do only one thing. Don't come to this holy place as a tourist. Come as a child visiting your father. Don't compare. Don't chatter. Don't socialize. Don't waste a moment.

I found it was easier to concentrate on the words of the prayers. I could express my deepest yearnings without being distracted. I wasn't wondering whether anyone was looking at me. As I said the *Amidah* of *Shacharis* I heard the birds singing. I knew that the sun had just come up and the entire world was now born anew. I felt like a new person.

I went to a shul where I had no connections and found new connections with Hashem.

An Answered Prayer

Bitachon — trust or faith — develops in you when you think about it. With a bit of effort you can find many opportunities to sing to Hashem every day. Rabbi Eliezer Papo, in his *sefer, Pele*

Yo'eitz, describes the benefits of faith: "When you look at life with open eyes you perceive how Hashem is supporting and guiding each person. This will develop your enthusiasm for mitzvos and you will take greater precautions to remain pure from sin. You will gain a lion's boldness for Hashem's service. Nothing will stop you because you will feel in your heart that Hashem is with you. Hashem sees, Hashem hears and the good you do is recorded and remembered. You will have complete faith. You will understand that when it is difficult to perform a good deed its reward is greater."

⚬〜⚬

It was an experience that filled you up. You felt overwhelmed with gratitude. You couldn't stop smiling. You tried to tell everyone the good news and to share the spark. Over and over again you marveled, "It's a miracle! This experience changed my life forever." You thought at the time that you would never feel discouraged again. Your feet felt light. Hashem answered your prayers. Ordinary things seemed more beautiful — the flowers, grass and trees; the blue sky seemed to glow. Now it's a year later and you wonder, where did that feeling go?

So many thoughts swirled through your mind. Miracles make us feel hopeful, happy, and uplifted. When a miracle occurs a voice within us whispers, "Hashem listens to all our prayers." Pondering wonderful news makes all our hopes more concrete. I've seen people who were extremely discouraged because of problems they could not solve. They seemed to have forgotten what a smile feels like. Then they see a newborn baby. A delicious spark of hope lights up their face as they smile at the baby. As David HaMelech said, "Hashem's strength is reflected in the babbling of a newborn child."

I've always wanted to have a sister. I wanted to share my room with someone and giggle with her at night. I wanted company. When I was young, I begged my parents for a sister to join me when I quarreled with my bother. I needed someone to help me make a battle plan. Wouldn't it be great to have someone who would be willing to play with dolls and collect stationery? I wanted a sister badly.

As I matured, I realized that if I wanted a sister Hashem is the One to ask, so I began praying fervently. By that time I was already in the fifth grade and my reasons had changed.

A sister can help you grow. You can share a secret with your sister and she won't laugh at you. Who is closer to you than a best friend? Since at that time I didn't even have a best friend, I really needed a sister. Therefore, every day when I prayed I begged for a sister.

Hashem answered my prayers. In the beginning of the seventh grade I found out the exciting news that my mother was expecting a baby. The youngest child in my family was 8 and everyone was ecstatic. I secretly prayed and wished for a healthy baby girl.

On 20 Nissan, April 27, I became a big sister. My sister is 5 years old now and she is the best sister I could have ever asked for.

Simi S.

❧

*O*ne blade of grass in a sea of green stood there trembling. She felt the fear of freezing and then, slowly, dying. This one blade of grass, along with all the others in the big, cold world, stood pleading with all its might for some warmth and protection.

Standing there trembling, she let her imagination flow. She remembered the warm summer months when the sun beat down on her. She recalled the sounds of children playing. She longed for a visit from her flower-friends. She remembered the time when there was no intense fear and shivering. She recalled all the long days she would spend just relaxing and growing tall and strong. She dreamed wistfully of those not-so-long-ago days.

Suddenly she noticed something different. Perched on her tip was a crystal-like beautifully shaped snowflake! More and more snowflakes began falling down, covering her completely. She could not see her friends now and she wondered what they were thinking.

She began feeling something vaguely familiar—warmth! The blade of grass was overjoyed. Her prayers were answered. Now she would be protected from the cold. With a grateful prayer of thanks, she dozed off into a peaceful slumber.

Basya D.

*I*t is Yom Kippur at night. I am babysitting while my mother goes to shul. At the moment the children are quiet, so I open my machzor to grab a few moments of prayer.

I sit in the dining room, holding my leather machzor and praying. Out of the corner of my eye I notice my 7-year-old sister standing in the corner swaying back and forth. I see that she is holding her own prayerbook. She is concentrating intently. Her dark hair falls over her small face as she carefully mouths each word.

I stand up and say each word slowly. When I finish, my sister is still swaying back and forth in the corner. I close my machzor. A moment later, my sister tenderly kisses her prayer book and places it near mine. With shining eyes she informs me, "We prayed till Hashem!"

Shaindy S.

*W*ay back in 1974, my aunt and uncle got married. Their wedding was a joyous occasion, with many people sharing in the celebration. My uncle learned in kollel and my aunt was a pre-school teacher. Several years passed but they remained childless.

Infertility led them on a very long and painful journey. They went to many doctors and tried several surgeries. Many rabbanim were consulted, brachos were given, but still they remained childless. One Torah sage suggested the segulah of living in Eretz Yisrael and visiting the Kosel and praying there for forty consecutive days. They went and prayed and poured out their hearts. One day a Kabbalist told them to buy a silver cup and inscribe it with the name David Moshe.

Fifteen years passed from their wedding day. Twenty years passed. They continued to pray and trust. They did not give up. Each time they heard of a new doctor they made an appointment. It was an emotional roller coaster. They confronted each stage of their ordeal with high hopes, only to have them crash down again. Many people told them, "Enough already! Don't torture yourselves. Your students, nieces and nephews are your children." However, they never gave up. One day Hashem would answer their prayers and put a child of their own in their arms.

After twenty-four years of marriage they heard of a doctor in Eretz Yisrael, Doctor Moshiach. After gathering their medical records they flew to Eretz Yisrael for a consultation. While reviewing their history the doctor said, "I give you a 10-percent chance of success. Go home. Don't waste your time and money." My uncle firmly replied that even if there is a 1-percent chance they will make the attempt. Everything is in Hashem's hands.

Miraculously my aunt gave birth to triplets, a boy and two girls, a year later! They are the sweetest, cutest, most adorable children you have ever seen. Family and friends wept with joy at their birth. The boy's bris was on Pesach, attended by over a hundred people.

For the first few months my aunt and uncle stayed with a close friend. Triplets are a challenge, to say the least. My family and I went over frequently to help at feeding time. After three months they returned to their own apartment. On Erev Yom Tov my aunt decided to polish her silver. Suddenly she came across a forgotten silver cup that she had purchased fifteen years earlier. It was inscribed with the name Dovid Moshe. This is her son's name. I still can't believe it!

The triplets are now 19 months old. They are walking, talking and getting into trouble at triple speed. I can't get enough of their company.

How wondrous and how great are the ways of Hashem. If we all had such bitachon in Hashem how many of our prayers would be answered!

Devorah Leba A.

Chapter 5

The Gift of Kindness

So Small But So Large

The phone rang again and again. I ran in and hurriedly put my packages down. Surrounded by a sea of grocery bags, I reached for the phone. That's when I heard the news that my relative was ill. Next week surgery would be performed in a Manhattan hospital. I stood there surrounded by the groceries for a party that would now have to be canceled. I felt lost and alone.

A week later, I called the Bikur Cholim. The surgery was over and now I wanted to visit my relative. Mount Sinai is a long train ride from Brooklyn. If I had a ride I'd be able to spend more time there. I would get a babysitter to stay with my 4 month old. Someone I had never met before offered to take me in her car on her way to work. When the car stopped on my corner I noticed that it was full.

A woman was sitting in the front; a nurse, a mother and child were in the back, and a pair of crutches lay on the floor. I squeezed into the back seat.

The car proceeded toward Fort Hamilton Parkway. Soon we were at the tollbooth. As our car went through the tunnel we all enjoyed an animated conversation with the driver. She made everyone feel like a personal friend, not like someone accepting a favor. The car stopped in midtown Manhattan at N.Y.U. Medical Center. The driver hopped out, opened her trunk and pulled out a wheelchair. She pushed the wheelchair to the front and gently helped the passenger into the wheelchair. She asked repeatedly, "Do you have everything you need?" When the woman was settled the nurse sitting in the back climbed out at a leisurely pace to push the wheelchair. Throughout it all, our driver was patient and caring.

The next stop was at Lenox Hill Hospital for the mother and child. Finally we reached Mount Sinai. I thanked her profusely. As I was about to exit the car, amazed over what I had just witnessed, I again thanked the gracious person who drove us all. I'll never forget her response:

"You really don't have to thank me. I didn't make a special trip today to take you to the hospital."

"I guess so," I said. "However, you were so gracious and patient with everyone who came in your car today and I think it's fabulous."

"Well," she replied, "I'm just extremely fortunate. I have to drive to work anyway. G-d gave me the opportunity to help people on the way. That's what makes me happy for the entire day."

I climbed out with a new understanding of gratitude. Her patience and gentle smile spoke volumes. She actually was appreciative not because of something she had received but because of something she had given to others. I felt hopeful and my heart was lighter as I walked toward the tall hospital building. "I have problems, but I also have people around me who care," I thought, and I felt really cheerful. When you see that level of pleasant helpfulness it gives you reason to be optimistic. This wonderful woman was truly happy with her lot, and her joy overflowed in the cheerful and royal manner in which she helped others.

Some people succeed in doing routine acts of kindness in an extraordinary way. I realize now that this helpful gesture of driving patients to the hospital is very potent. It can immeasurably strengthen the spirit of the recipients and even hasten their recovery. Help with the small details is encouraging, because what may seem like a minor detail to one person is often a major obstacle for another.

When we feel hopeful, we interact with other people in a positive, optimistic manner. People are attracted by our energy. They are drawn to us and enjoy spending time at our side. They know we will listen to them, smile and be encouraging. This in turn brings out the best in people, creating a supportive atmosphere all around. We feel that we have something to give to others when we are filled with hopeful thoughts.

An insignificant incident can mean so much. It is truly a diamond that you take with you through life.

Ticket To Happiness

In kindergarten we learned that we have to share with others. Sometimes we did so reluctantly, breaking a potato chip in half before offering a piece to a friend. Now, we have changed. Now that we are older, we not only know how to give but we look for the chance to do so. While rushing through our routine, sometimes we stumble upon a wonderful opportunity. On our way to accomplish an errand we may notice something our friend or sibling needs. We might see a meter maid on the block and drop a quarter into a stranger's meter. A friend we haven't seen for a while is shopping at the grocery. She suggests a *shidduch* and we hastily exchange phone numbers.

As we have grown we have learned that when we extend ourselves to others, the act of caring benefits us as much as it does our friends. When we open our eyes, many occasions for giving appear before us. The following experience was an opportunity that I did not plan in advance. I could call it a gift because so much pleasure came my way that evening.

I had purchased four concert tickets three months in advance because I wanted to get good seats at the school's performance. On the Thursday before the performance there was a change in plans and

I realized that I had an extra ticket. What should I do? I didn't feel bad about the ticket's cost, because the money would benefit the school. Yet it seemed a shame to waste three hours of potential enjoyment.

I had an idea. I called a relative and told her about the concert on *Motza'ei Shabbos.* "I have an extra ticket," I said. "Please join us. I'll pick you up and bring you home. I'd enjoy having your company during the concert."

The relative was enthusiastic. "It sounds like a wonderful idea. When should I be ready?"

We squeezed into my small black car and began the twisting and turning drive to the concert. It was fun to chat with my relative on the way. It made the 20-minute ride pass quickly. My children enjoyed their friends in the backseat.

We sat in the darkened room and watched the concert. We cried during the sad parts and laughed at the humorous skits. The time flew by. Suddenly the entire cast was on stage in their colorful costumes singing the finale with gusto.

It was three hours of pleasure. My enjoyment was definitely doubled this year. I had shared it and that had made all the difference.

∽ා࿐

*F*ive friends once went to a restaurant together. After placing *their orders, they began chatting among themselves. When the waiter came back with the first course, they ignored him and continued talking. However, one person in the group paused for a few seconds and said two simple words — "Thank you."*

The main course was served. The same thing happened. The group disregarded the waiter but one person paused and said, "This is so kind of you."

The group decided to order dessert. When they were served they noticed that each of them received one scoop of ice cream but the person who said "thank you" received two.

In surprise they asked their friend if she knew the waiter. The friend replied, "Actually, I've never met him before. However there is one thing that I know about him. He's a human being read the first verse. Our teacher read the verse and explained it. Afterward she turned to the class, "Would anyone like to read the first verse for the first time?"

Many hands went up. We were all eager to read that first verse of Navi. Suddenly I heard my teacher call my name. I was thrilled! I could not believe that out of all the girls in the class I had been chosen.

It was a good feeling. I felt my heart lift as I carefully read that verse. I still remember every word of it. I felt exceptional.

My teacher praised me heartily, "Great, excellent, well done!" Now I'm about to graduate and I still feel those complimentary words. They are like sunshine on my back.

Words mean so much. They can have a positive effect on a person. This is a teacher I will always think of fondly.

Shoshana Z.

∽১৶

❧ *The First Time*

With a feeling of anxiety I pushed the "6" button on the elevator. The elevator glided up six flights while picking up and dropping off various passengers. Then I arrived at the sixth floor. The doors slid open. The beeps of the monitors greeted me, causing my heart to skip a beat. But nonetheless I put my right foot forward, determined to continue. I entered the large communal dining room and glanced around. Nausea hit me. One 85-year-old man was demanding in an overly loud voice, "Sugar, sugar for my coffee …" I looked away before I could see the blind woman on my right. Another man was rolling his head back and forth with drool dripping from his mouth.

I felt an urge to leave. Then a nurse said, "Can you please feed this gentleman?" I swallowed hard, and tried to answer in a calm voice, "Sure."

Metropolitan was serving vegetable soup for lunch. I took a spoon of the chunky vegetable soup and brought it slowly to the man's mouth. Half of it dripped onto his white plastic bib. My second spoonful disappeared without any spills. Another spoon came and went. I was getting better at it. We finished the soup. The next thing on his tray was the bread. Was I supposed to feed the bread to my gentleman? Who knows if he can chew it? I did not want anyone to choke now (especially not on my first try!).

After a while someone explained that the bread should be dipped in coffee in order to soften it. Next I found a banana on the serving tray. I don't particularly like bananas. Mashing the bananas doesn't really improve the taste, appearance or texture. I put on a brave front and I fed this man some banana. It wasn't so bad after all.

It was finally time to leave. So, I smiled at the gentleman I had been feeding and told him, "Have a great day, Sir." He smiled contentedly back at me. I knew I had done a great job.

I came to school knowing that "I" wasn't the only focus of my day. These elderly are a link between the past and the present. When these people can smile, despite their troubles, I can surely smile too.

Tehila K.

❧ Kindness Notebook

A simple way to motivate yourself to become a better person is to keep a record of your minor acts of kindness. It's an easy daily habit that has far-reaching effects.

A regular notebook becomes elevated when it is used to record acts of kindness. Each night think about the past day and try to remember your minor acts of kindness and record them. Now your notebook has become a "kindness notebook."

The kindness notebook makes you a better person. Decide that you simply cannot go to sleep unless you have done at least one kind deed today. The notebook is on your mind throughout the day. It reminds you to act in a caring and sharing manner. If you persist in writing in your notebook every day you will become a better person.

Esty O.

Make this notebook even more special by purchasing it together with a friend. You can have a great time decorating the notebooks for each other on a free afternoon. You may want to use pretty pictures, stickers, or souvenirs of things you've done together. This will help both of you feel eager to write in the kindness notebook.

～ↄબ

Receiving nourishes the body but giving nourishes the soul. Every person who shared their story with me discovered that acts of kindness bring lasting joy to the GIVER. Doing an act of kindness for another is a gift you give to yourself.

he wanted them. The angels cooked and served the food. It was only after the sin of partaking of the fruit of the Tree of Knowledge that man had to struggle and worry about providing for tomorrow.

Hashem still provides. I know it's true, but I often forget. After every detail falls into place I'll gratefully say that Hashem gave it all to me. However, when I face a difficult decision I often don't know what to do. What will happen? A solution involves an investment of time and effort, yet it's still hard to decide if you have done enough. However, one day a week you can step back and say, "Hashem will provide." It's a reassuring knowledge on which we all can rely. On Shabbos we can be completely calm, happy and truly optimistic. On Shabbos we can draw strength from our faith and not dwell on our problems. One lesson of Shabbos is that sustenance comes from Heaven.

When did our food literally come from heaven? The manna that Hashem provided for the Jewish people in the Wilderness came the closest to the state of mankind in Gan Eden. It literally came from the skies. Although everyone had to go out and gather the manna each day, and couldn't save it from one day to the next, no work was involved in its production. The concept of work providing sustenance did not apply then. Hashem sustained us and it was a true *brachah*. One way this was evident was that those who collected more came home with the same amount as those who collected less.

This occurred during the six days of the week, but Shabbos was different. No work was necessary to provide for Shabbos. Even the minor effort of going out and collecting the manna was unnecessary. Shabbos was like Gan Eden. On the sixth day they collected a double portion. Rashi explains that each person collected the same amount as usual but when he came home he found that Hashem had given him a surprise gift — the manna was double the usual measure. Although one could not save manna for the following day during the week because it spoiled, on Shabbos the extra portion of manna stayed perfectly fresh.

Every Shabbos we enjoy the same gift that the generation in the Wilderness enjoyed. Shabbos is a time of freedom. It means freedom from toil, worry and stress. Shabbos brought blessing then and it continues to bring blessing now.

A Special Day —
Hashem's Brachah

Shabbos is a day that enhances our feeling of well-being. On Shabbos we sing the praises of Hashem and this music fills our ears and enters our soul. The rich scent of tasty Shabbos foods cures listlessness and brings joy. The well-prepared foods, the freshly baked challah, the pretty flowers can counteract depression. The ideas we take time to study on Shabbos awaken our senses. We remember our glorious past, connect with our magnificent present, and feel part of a future that we pray will be even better than we are anticipating. The curse of worry does not affect Shabbos at all. On Shabbos you don't worry. On Shabbos we are Hashem's guests.

This is what *Chazal* say about Hillel: Hillel declared, "*Baruch Hashem yom yom*, Blessed is Hashem every day." He did not worry about providing for Shabbos. He was certain that he was Hashem's guest and that Hashem would provide every delight for Shabbos. Each week, Hashem provided a nice animal for Hillel so that he would have meat for Shabbos. Hillel didn't worry and didn't exert extra effort for this. When he needed it, it was somehow made available for him.

Did this happen only for Hillel or does it happen to ordinary people in our times?

Can we also have this feeling that Hashem is guiding our steps and providing for our Shabbos?

Can we see in our lives that our efforts to make Shabbos special bear extraordinary fruits?

Can we see today in our humble lives that Hashem is taking care of us and we shouldn't worry?

❧

The following incident appeared in the newspaper *Hamodia*. Every other week's paper features a story that underscores Divine providence. I usually turn to this section as soon as the paper falls through the mail slot. The stories reinforce the message that miracles occur every day. I always feel uplifted by the serendipitous events about which I read. I feel protected, because these stories confirm that Hashem is always with the Jewish nation and He is taking care of each individual. It's as if my worries are a voice playing in my head and after reading these particular stories that voice is muffled.

●◆ Gefilte Fish

*M*y son and his family live in one of the outlying religious communities. His wife, in addition to working part-time, manages a household blessed with children, cooks, cleans, shops and keeps a smile on her face most of the time. She is also in charge of the family finances.

One recent Thursday, she discovered that they had somehow gone over their monthly budget and would have to economize drastically until the beginning of the new month. My daughter-in-law was relieved to find that she had everything she needed for the Shabbos meals in the freezer — except for gefilte fish. She decided to make a tuna fish salad for Shabbos and add lots of cut-up vegetables to make it go around as a replacement for the gefilte fish.

On Friday night, when the men left for shul, my daughter-in-law took the children with her to visit a friend. As she walked home, she began to regret that she was going to serve plain week-day tuna fish on Shabbos. My son would undoubtedly ask her why they were having tuna instead of gefilte fish, and she would have to tell him about the state of their finances. "How much would a bit of gefilte fish have cost after all?" she asked herself.

She realized that it was too late to do anything about it and decided to make the best of the situation. She would bravely face her disappointed husband and they would just have to eat tuna fish.

As she reached her front door, a neighbor's child arrived and handed her a covered dish. "My mommy sent you this." The dish contained six large portions of cooked gefilte fish.

How had her neighbor known that she was wishing for gefilte fish to serve on Shabbos? My daughter-in-law was so astonished *with the unexpected delivery that she asked no questions and took advantage of her well-intentioned neighbor's largesse.*

A few days later the mystery was cleared up. That particular neighbor was one of a group of women who had cooked various dishes to send to a Mrs. D. who was sick and could not make Shabbos for her family. When the child returned home and told his mother that he had delivered the fish as requested to Mrs. E., the mistake was discovered. Naturally another dish of fish was sent off immediately to Mrs. D.

"So you see," my daughter-in-law ended her tale, "Hashem takes care of us right down to the gefilte fish for Shabbos."

❦

R' Chaim Shmulevitz brings another lesson from the manna.

When the Jews came home from gathering the manna that first Friday and saw that it had doubled before their eyes, they were surprised. They went to Moshe and inquired, "Why did this miracle happen? Why has the manna suddenly become a double portion?"

Moshe explained, "At the beginning of the week Hashem informed me about this. Hashem is giving you a gift for Shabbos. You received a double portion today because on Shabbos you don't have to worry or gather food."

If Moshe knew about Shabbos from the first day of the week why didn't he tell *Bnei Yisrael* what to expect? Why did he wait until they went out to gather the manna on Friday and discovered the bonus portion? The Rashbam explains that Moshe purposely didn't tell them about the double portion — the gift of Shabbos — in advance because he wanted *Bnei Yisrael* to feel that Shabbos is special. Had he informed them of the miracle that was to happen on Friday, the people would have become accustomed to the idea over the week. In that case they wouldn't have felt as inspired by the miracle. They would not have realized that Shabbos is a precious gift. Therefore, it was worthwhile for Moshe to postpone telling them the prophecy concerning Shabbos so that *Bnei Yisrael* would receive a surprise gift. This would be an impressive and powerful miracle that the Jewish nation would always remember — Shabbos is a blessed day. Shabbos is a gift.

∽◦∾

Perhaps it is our task now and in the future to endow Shabbos with a feeling of celebration. Shabbos is a gift. How can this be demonstrated? When we bake a delicious cake or *kugel* to honor Shabbos, and when we set the table with beautiful dishes, and when we dress in honor of Shabbos *all* the time — not just when we go out, but even when we are staying home — this makes the Shabbos day a gift for us and for our families.

Handmade With Love

The Shabbos tablecloth catches your eye when you enter the kitchen and brings a smile to your lips. It reminds you of an English garden in the spring. The tablecloth has an uplifting color scheme. The roses are shades of maroon, ruby, scarlet and pink and the leaves are several shades of green, olive and emerald. Occasionally when I have zipped through the Friday marathon, I've spread out this tablecloth on the wrong side and even so it looked quite good. Only at second glance does one realize the error.

This tablecloth was a gift that we enjoy every Shabbos. It is special because my aunt stitched by hand every single cross-stitch that decorates the fabric. I can visualize my aunt sitting on her porch with the tablecloth spread out on a little bridge table in front of her. She explained, "I often do embroidery outside. In the sunshine the illumination is best and I can see colors clearly." My aunt doesn't just push a needle up and down through the fabric according to the pattern someone else designed. She creates her own personal masterpiece. A lot of thought and creativity was invested to make this handmade tablecloth a work of fine art.

The shading is carefully planned. My aunt measures precise pieces of each thread so that each color is used in the exact amount necessary. Where most people would be content with one color for the roses, Lina incorporates four or five shades of red and pink into the flower.

The tablecloth reminds me of a woman short in stature with a big heart. I can picture her sitting on her patio in Florida and stitching away at the tablecloth on her lap. Every day she goes out to work in the morning sun so that the shading will be perfect. I can see her smile as she anticipates giving the gift when it is complete.

The Shabbos tablecloth is more than a work of art, it's a work of love.

Don't Worry

If you are like me, you sometimes wake up in the morning with an uneasy feeling in your stomach. It's an unpleasant knot of tension somewhere near the lower side of your abdomen. I wish it weren't there. I've heard so many lessons about faith and trust. I just wish I could tell them to my stomach.

This message plays in my head, "You should be doing better. You should be doing more."

Shabbos is a day to find freedom from that voice. On Shabbos you don't have to do, you simply have to be. On Shabbos you aren't permitted to plan. Shabbos is an island of calm in the stormy sea of the workweek. Shabbos reminds us that Hashem is guiding the world.

Hashem created the world and He creates it anew every day. Shabbos reminds us that for six days Hashem created the world and on the seventh day He rested.

A young girl was going on a long bus ride. She sat up front. She felt nervous because it was her first time on the bus by herself. She sat right behind the driver's seat. Suddenly the driver stopped the bus and ran out to get a cup of coffee. The young girl looked at the wheel. In her mind it seemed to be spinning out of control. She panicked and was sure the bus was moving. "Oh, no! I'm lost! The bus will just move on its own and I'll never get to Netanya to see my aunt," she thought to herself. A few moments passed. The driver returned. The young girl relaxed. Someone *is* driving the bus. She will get to Netanya safely.

We are all riding a "bus" in this world. Sometimes we panic. However, on Shabbos we can take the time to remember that there is always a Guiding Force controlling the wheel. Shabbos helps us put things in perspective.

1. Stop — make time for compassion and for togetherness.

2. Hashem knows what you need. Hashem provides. Hashem will take care.

3. Don't worry. There is a higher plan. Hashem is guiding the world.

4. Take time to make Shabbos special. It will ensure your success.

When we light the Shabbos candles the next 25 hours begin. They are expanded in every way. There is a powerful energy in the day that affects every part of the individual, the family and the Jewish nation. Remember that no problem is insurmountable because Hashem is giving us strength. Shabbos reminds us that we can transcend our circumstances. Each week the two loaves of challah commemorate the miracle of the manna and remind us of the gift of Shabbos. They remind us that we do not have to worry, because Shabbos will bring blessing. They remind us that we are part of a glorious history, and an even more magnificent future awaits us.

Melaveh Malkah

Many people think that the *Melaveh Malkah* meal is less important than the other meals with which we celebrate Shabbos. Reb Shloime taught that this meal is perhaps the most important because during *Melaveh Malkah* we connect the holiness of Shabbos to the ordinary weekdays.

What is *Melaveh Malkah* supposed to be like? Do we somehow bring the holiness of Shabbos into the week? How do we access holiness? Do we have to be surrounded by many people? Do we have to listen to specific music? There are so many questions. It's easier to feel serenity on Shabbos because most activities that we are busy with during the week stop. There are no phones, computers, fax machines, or cars to distract us. However, *Motza'ei Shabbos* is a challenge. As soon as we make *Havdalah* the tasks and worries of the week begin to creep in. The phone rings, there is homework, housework, etc. Pressures of the week immediately assail us. What can we do to transfer the holiness and faith of Shabbos into our week?

Reb Shloime might have been sitting alone in his small kitchen, yet from deep within his heart he was able to generate serenity and closeness to Hashem. He didn't need to be in the company of others for this. He didn't need a crowd. He could evoke this feeling from within. I was there as an observer. I just watched.

It was *Motza'ei Shabbos*. I sat in Reb Shloime's house in the Mattersdorf section of Yerushalayim for *Melaveh Malkah*. He said, "Believe me, I'm not eating because I'm hungry, I'm eating in honor of the *seudah* of *Melaveh Malkah*."

He sat at his small table off the kitchen and sang a familiar traditional *Melaveh Malkah* song. The song describes a chassid — a man of great devotion — who was very poor. His wife begged him to find a means of sustenance for her and their five children. The man meets Eliyahu HaNavi who says, "Sell me as a slave for 800,000 gold coins ..."

Reb Shloime sang this song and it felt like the chassid was sitting there at that small table. He sang about the 800,000 gold coins and they were glittering on that small table.

Reb Shloime is absolutely the wealthiest man I know — not in material terms but in things which are far more important. He knows without a doubt where to find that which is most fundamental. His life overflows with the essential ingredients of a life full of satisfaction each and every day.

He sits and rocks and sings. His eyes are closed and his heart swells with the song. It's so powerful it frightens me. I find it difficult to comprehend this type of greatness. His soul, mind, limbs and the entire room are suffused with the song. It's so complete and real.

I miss that experience so much. I do the same things that Reb Shloime does, but 80 percent of me is somewhere else. Was he singing or listening? Yes, he began the song, but there was "something" more that followed. I've never seen that "something" at any other *Melaveh Malkah*.

It's the intensity and the entirety of it that I've never seen duplicated elsewhere. It was so fervent. It came from deep within and it permeated the atmosphere. The rhythm, the tone, the words, the concentration on his face were other-worldly. This was the real thing.

His singing was so sincere. He wasn't performing the song. When he finished the *zemiros* he would look up and seem rather surprised that someone was there.

Reb Shloime is not a rabbi. Over the years, he has worked at different businesses. Now he must be 80, may he have many healthy years. For the past twenty-five years, he's been learning. He knows how to learn. The rosh yeshivah in the neighborhood is his *chavrusa*. He manages three different *gemach* funds from his home. His greatest joy is doing acts of kindness. Reb Shloime is simply a real Jew, an inspiration to those fortunate enough to know him.

The gift of Shabbos is bestowed upon us every week. It is up to us to appreciate it and make the most of this blessed day. We also are blessed with many holidays throught the year, and some of us even have our favorite ones. When Yamim Tovim take on an added significance and we realize how they enrich our lives every day of the year, we know that we have grown.

●❖ *Simchas Torah*

*S*pecial moments. Moments flash by and disappear as rapidly as a streak of lightning. Yet somewhere inside me they will remain forever. These are the moments that keep me going and make me smile when I feel down.

Simchas Torah is a time to rejoice. This year I spent this holiday in Skver. I stood on the crowded bleachers and waited. I felt a mixture of emotions. I'm ashamed to admit that I felt irritated at first. Hundreds of ladies, girls and young children crowded *together. We stood sideways, hands pinned to our sides. The aggressive ones pushed forward, leaned over and spread out their hands even though there was no room. An array of sounds and smells tickled my ears and nose. Small children ran around shouting gaily. Bags of candy, flags and toy Torahs were clutched tightly in their grubby palms. There were babies lying in carriages dressed in their Yom Tov finery. Some were kicking happily and some cried. The various textures of my neighbors' outfits brushed against me. Tweed, wool and fur rubbed against me from all four directions. However, I knew that this discomfort was not important.*

The reason we were squeezed in this small space and feeling mounting excitement was because of what was happening down below. In the men's section below the women's balcony the bleachers hugged all four walls, forming an empty rectangle. The men stood on them, crowded together, divided by age. All eyes looked to the center of the room where a small wooden shtender was positioned. Poised by the shtender and learning softly was the Rebbe. Though his back was facing me I could sense the holiness.

The Rebbe picked up his small Sefer Torah and began walking slowly, followed by several chosen men, also carrying Sifrei Torah. Like soldiers marching after their general, the men followed their Rebbe step by step. After circling the room, the men slowly dispersed and the Rebbe positioned himself once again in front of the shtender.

The Rebbe began praying loudly, one line at a time. The massive audience repeated each line after him. The chassidim, all dressed in white shirts, long black coats, and black beaver hats, began singing in unison. After a few minutes of song the Rebbe began tapping his feet. This was the climax. All the men began singing louder, thundering praise to the Almighty. With hands clasped they moved back and forth like piano keys. The floors shook, the ceiling reverberated with the echo of their joyful dancing.

A holy glow radiated from the Rebbe's face. He danced alone around the large room, stamping his feet. The joy was mirrored on the faces of the thousands of men dancing along.

This ceremony was repeated seven times. At the culmination, the Rebbe's voice proclaimed three times, "Next year in Yerushalayim!" The chassidim fervently swayed back and forth at the mention of these holy words. They repeated them slowly, in tune, concentration etched on their faces. Suddenly they burst into song with energy and joy. They jumped higher and higher, reaching toward the heavens.

My heart soared as I watched this magnificent sight. This was a prayer in song. It was a plea to the Almighty. Hashem, we are ready; take us now to Jerusalem. My soul felt the sorrow and longing too. On this night of Simchas Torah we rejoiced with the Torah and we hope and pray that next year we will dance in Jerusalem.

Esti R.

Chapter 7

The Gift of Self-Esteem

• Inspiration

• Resolution

You Don't Have to Do It All

When we remain calm Hashem's Presence dwells in our home.

We've discussed many benefits that will enter your life if you have a positive view of life. It's just as vital to have a positive view of *you*. It's important to see yourself in a positive light. Why is it easier to remember our mistakes instead of our successes? We often think we aren't good enough. It's so easy to fall into the whirlpool of sad, discouraging thoughts. Emotional trauma comes when we least expect it. We may encounter a difficult person, worry about accomplishing a specific task, or compare our performance to someone else's tremendous success. Without warning we feel a tension in our jaw and an ache in our stomach. We feel that we're in terrible danger and our body creates the symptoms to support that feeling. Basic needs such as getting healthy nourishment and adequate sleep are set aside. This compounds our feelings of inadequacy.

Do you need to achieve success in order to survive? Whether it's an exam in school, a performance, a gala event or any other goal, is perfection really the most important part of the equation? After the "test" will you wake up and wonder, "Was that really so important? Was it worth making myself sick over it?"

The great secret of developing self-esteem is this: There isn't any secret. You don't have to go to a special place, do a heroic deed, buy an expensive item or improve your technique to access the feeling that you are precious. Being happy with who you are is simply a matter of choice — starting now. I learned this from my upstairs neighbor, Nenie, when I was married for about six months and obsessed with the goal of becoming the perfect cook.

"Nenie" is Hungarian for aunt and Nenie was the perfect aunt to everyone. She took care of all her friends and neighbors. She encouraged, gave lavish compliments, and helped you see the positive aspects of every problem. Her advice was often offered along with a delicious treat.

Nenie knew how to cook and bake very well. I visited often and tried to pick up some hints. I watched her magical hands dice onions, knead dough, measure ingredients and fry cutlets. Her cutlets never stuck to the pan, her food never burned, her *kugel* was the perfect texture and her *kokosh* cake tasted like paradise.

One Shabbos morning, I sat in her kitchen surrounded by the delicious scent of *chulent* as we talked about food. I told Nenie how excited I was about a complicated *kugel* recipe I had mastered. After six months of marriage the *kugel* finally came out good. She told me, "You listen to an old lady. If it's too hard for you to make it from scratch you don't have to do it." I told her that I've always wanted to be an expert cook. She talked about *kokosh* cake. She'd been making homemade *kokosh* cake for thirty years, every single week. I told her that I had never met someone who could make a really good *kokosh* cake before. Then she taught me a lesson I never forgot. She said:

"I was leaving for Florida in two days. Several crises arose that just had to be taken care of, so I had a lot of unexpected work. I did not have a moment to myself. There were many things I couldn't leave half-finished prior to my trip. Before I turned around it was Wednesday noon. Since my plane was leaving at 6 p.m., I realized I wouldn't have enough time to bake and freeze the *kokosh* cake for my husband. So I went to the bakery and bought four *kokosh* cakes. I brought them home, sliced them, wrapped them in foil and put them in the freezer.

"A week later my husband called me in Florida and told me, 'Your *kokosh* cake is better than ever before.' I looked back at all the times I had pushed myself beyond my limits to make that homemade *kokosh* cake. Listen to me. A lady doesn't have to be a superwoman. Do what you can, but don't think you have to do it all. You are precious just the way you are."

I laughed and reflected on the ways in which we seem compelled to accomplish a goal, yet sometimes it's not even that important. We want everything to be perfect, even extraordinary. In the meantime, we feel frazzled, impatient and fatigued. Nenie was telling me that it's okay to be human, it's okay to ask for help, and it's okay to keep things simple. One doesn't have to do it all.

Eventually, I learned that when you don't feel under pressure to be perfect a Divine spark ignites inside you. This may come as a surprise because you may have always thought that only painful struggle leads to success. As the cliché goes, "No pain, no gain." Sometimes there is something you think of doing and it just calls to you, so you decide to try it just for fun without worrying about the outcome. Frequently, the results are much better than you expected. Perhaps you experienced this when you took a cooking class just for fun. The recipe seemed complicated, but you weren't worried since this was just your first time trying it. At the end, the results were almost professional, and you stood back and smiled.

It's much easier to be your best self when you are aware that however things turn out you'll be okay. If we allow ourselves some leeway our thoughts, creativity and intuition may surprise us. The pressure is reduced and it feels as though a 40-pound weight is lifted off our back. Our attitude toward everyone and everything is better when we stop trying to be perfect. Your best is good enough. When you stop pushing yourself beyond endurance things usually turn out better than you thought they would.

Complete the following sentences with the first thought that comes to your mind. Remember to think good thoughts. Exercise your imagination! If you believe it 50 percent, Hashem can surely make it real.

I am really good at:

1. _____

2. _____

3. _____

I enjoy doing:

1. _____

2. _____

3. _____

I have the ability to:

1. _____

2. _____

3. _____

I am giving myself time to learn how to:

1. _____

2. _____

3. _____

One way to awaken feelings of assurance is to remember our peak moments. This poem about graduation night helps me feel that I am right there.

Graduation Night

Waiting for the piano's slow musical tones,
Lining up in double file,
We advanced majestically
With just a hint of a smile.

I looked straight ahead
And touched my strand of pearls.
I took careful slow steps.
Tonight the door was opening
To the big wide world.

I sat on stage on graduation night.
The speaker's voice resounded
And filled the room.
I tried not to think about
My stage fright.

School was over and that was great,
I'd get my diploma and take a bow.
But I was anxious about my fate —
What would I do now?

I felt important as I walked back to my seat —
After hours of study,
After hundreds of tests,
I was finished with work —
Now could I rest?

It was then that I saw them,
They sat to the right —
I saw all my teachers,
They were proud of us tonight.

I saw their genuine smiles
And felt they wished us well.

They didn't have to be there,
But came because they care.

As I walked further,
Out of the corner of my eye
I saw my sister waving.
She took a picture as I passed by.

Finally I saw my mother,
Her eyes were shining so tonight.
She smiled at me through her tears
And I forgot my fears.

The piano sounded a long drawn-out chord,
In unison we faced in one direction.
As we waited for the second signal,
I saw the spectators leaning forward.
Hundreds of relatives had filled every chair,
They had come with best wishes —
That the sky we walk under
Always be fair.

Until that moment I had thought
That this was *my* graduation night.
However, now I realized
That notion just was not right.

The second chord echoed,
The graduates sat.
The principal spoke
Words of inspiration that glowed.

Tonight was my chance
To finally make a start
And say what's in my heart
To all those wonderful people here.

They gently helped me
Along the way,
Their wisdom guided me
Until I reached this day.

The ceremony ended,
But it wasn't too late —
I rushed past my acquaintances
To teachers and family
And mouthed two simple heartfelt words —
Thank you!

Holding on to Inspiration

My big sister is almost 12 years older than I am. We share a special bond. She gave me many opportunities to see exciting things. Once when I was 4 we went on the subway to Manhattan. I remember walking with my big sister on a busy Manhattan street. There were so many tall buildings. Even when I bent my head back and looked up I couldn't see the tops of the buildings. Streams of people surrounded us. The sidewalks were crowded. There were tables covered with black cloths. People sold scarves and jewelry. Someone called, "Just $5 for a designer scarf. It's right here. Come and have a look." The sky was dusky blue. We were walking to the subway.

We passed a black and white sign and blue stairs and I thought that was our train. My sister said, "No, we have to walk some more." I saw yellow taxis and huge busses whiz past. Someone's radio was playing loudly out of an open car window. "Hold on to your balloon," my sister warned. With one hand I held on to my sister because I didn't want to get lost in the crowd. With the other hand I held on to my helium balloon. I was determined not to lose this balloon. I wore my navy coat with the two rows of gold buttons and a hat made of the same fabric as the coat; the earflaps were tied under my chin.

We continued walking together. We saw a lady who looked funny with her red and blond hair mixed together. I knew I wanted to hold on to that balloon. My sister had offered to tie it to one of my buttons, but I would feel silly walking in the street like that. I was big and I could hold on to the balloon. I was watching it. Some cars began honking loudly. I almost jumped. I was mesmerized by the balloon's shape and color and the way it floated above me.

The balloon made no sound. No bells rang, no voice called, no siren wailed. There wasn't even a whisper. How did it slip out of my hand? Did someone jostle my arm? I didn't feel it become loose. Ah! Suddenly the balloon was floating out of reach. It seemed to rise slowly, yet it flew away before I could grab it back. I looked after it wistfully as it floated up into the sky. My balloon soared slowly up and out of reach. All I could do was gaze at it as it grew smaller and smaller.

I still had to pretend that I wasn't disappointed because I didn't want my sister to scold, "I told you to hold on to your balloon."

Life offers many opportunities for inspiration. We feel uplifted and we smile with satisfaction. However, that lofty feeling does not last; it soon floats away. It's difficult to hold on to our ideals. We want to remember those lessons we have learned when we are faced with a challenge. When occurrences cause us to fall short of our ideals how can we respond in a better way? How does one stay inspired?

What standards would we like to incorporate? Good deeds, developing oneself, inner harmony — all sound wonderful. But we often keep our resolutions for less than a week. We make a firm decision that from now on we will be different. Perhaps we declare our good intentions. Those first few days feel so good. Then we start thinking, "Get on with your life, you're not that bad. This is just too hard." On occasion we can have a day that we are really proud of, but it's difficult to live that way all the time. Yet deep inside we still yearn for meaningful days every day.

Judaism says that Hashem is our Father in Heaven and we are His children. Just like any parent, Hashem wants His children to succeed. Hashem wants our dreams to come true.

We are all willing to make self-improvements. Nevertheless, our ideals seem to slip away without even a warning whisper. Why?

If we are dedicated to an ideal it is always on our mind. Even when things seem impossible, we are constantly on the lookout for a possibility to do the right thing. Meyer Birnbaum was in the army during World War II. He was willing to work harder and walk a great distance to be among other religious Jews on Yom Kippur.

I was in Camp Edison. The High Holidays were drawing near, and the captain in charge of my group noticed on my records that I was a divinity student. Since there were no Jewish chaplains available, he asked me to lead the Rosh Hashanah prayers, which I did. The captain also asked me to lead the prayers for Yom Kippur, but this time I didn't accept immediately. I was friendly with him and decided to do a little bargaining.

"What's in it for me?" I asked him.

"What do you want?" he replied.

I had gotten to know Rabbi Abba Gewirtz, who later became the vice president of Telshe Yeshiva in Wickliffe, Ohio, and who at that time had a shul in Bradley Beach, and I requested permission to daven Neilah at his shul.

My request was granted. I explained to the captain that I could not carry a pass out of the base and that he should inform the Military Police along the way that I was allowed to travel without a pass to Bradley Beach. At camp, I led practically the entire Kol Nidrei, Maariv, Shacharis, Mussaf and Minchah davening with some help from another soldier. After Minchah, I headed towards Bradley Beach. At the outpost, the guard greeted me and asked if I was Private Birnbaum. Informed that I was, he told me that he would be looking out for me until I got to Bradley Beach.

The walk to Bradley Beach was several miles. When I entered the shul, Rabbi Gewirtz motioned for me to join him up front. That was the last thing I remember. When I awoke, a doctor in the rabbi's house was treating me, with his wife hovering anxiously nearby. The sudden contrast between the fresh air outside and the crowded stuffy shul — especially after fasting all day, leading the davening and the long walk — was too much for me and I had fainted as soon as I had entered the shul.

The Gift of Self-Esteem □ 99

Mayer Birnbaum was alone at an army base. There were many difficulties, especially for an Orthodox Jew. His deepest desire was to serve Hashem as well as possible and to do as many mitzvos as possible. When there was no one to lead the prayers, he did it. His one desire was to pray in a shul at least for *Neilah*. He walked several miles while fasting just to get to shul.

His yearning to do Hashem's will was always on his mind. Despite the challenges to his ideals, he persistently looked for ways to do things according to the Torah.

Often we expect to sail easily on the river of life. When we hit the rapids and our boat is pitched every which way, our ideals tend to drift away. There is always a gap between the stimulus that rocks our boat, challenging our ideals, and our reaction. Yet there is time to think before we speak or act. There is an opportunity to choose. What can help us to make the right choice? We want to insure that we continue on the path we intended to follow. There are some steps we can take:

Pray! — You can talk to Hashem in your own words wherever you are and whenever you wish. You can ask Hashem for help, for wisdom, for closeness to Him. You can ask Hashem for the big things and the small things.

Use Your Imagination — You can create in your mind the ideal you want to pursue. Take a moment when you first wake up to imagine that today you will keep your resolutions.

∾

When I was a child I loved to daydream and fantasize. An imagination has many magical powers. It can take you to the ocean, rolling over waves, or gliding on slippery ice, climbing plush green hills and walking through sunny meadows. I was the heroine of every war, the princess of each fairy tale, or the courageous bold knight who saved the king. In my fantasy world, I had the magic touch and a solution to every problem. How great is the power of imagination.

Leah H.

∾

A s a child I had a lively imagination. My reflection was my friend. The little girl in the mirror was my companion. I'd talk and smile and a "real person" smiled back. When I got older I realized it was me in the mirror. I also realized that I have to be my own best friend.

Chani K.

We often think that we can't use the power of imagination to actualize ideals because we just don't have an imagination. But if we think back to our younger years we will see that our imagination is very powerful. We can use this same ability to become inspired and face challenges.

Write!

- Find a quiet place where you know you won't be disturbed for at least 10 minutes, and write.

- You might want to play some music. You might want to let your mind wander for a few minutes. Then pick up a pen and write about your ideal.

- Write down why this particular ideal is important to you.

- Write about your dreams.

- Write about specific goals. Change your plans from "one of these days," to "tomorrow" or "next week" — don't keep postponing your dreams.

- Write down your small triumphs.

Use Your Free Will — Ask yourself: "What behaviors are enslaving me? What would life be like without them?" We all have the ability to act based on our knowledge and choice. Remember that you have the power to choose how you will behave.

- Our soul knows that we want to give and to help others.

- Our soul knows that we want to connect with Hashem.

- Our soul knows that we want to connect with other people in a meaningful way.

- Our soul knows that we can do more than we had ever dreamed was possible.

Take Each Day at a Reasonable Pace — Be gentle with yourself, regardless of what comes your way. Don't struggle against typical limitations. Pace yourself instead of pushing until you are exhausted. Settle for the best you can be right now. There may be many goals before you but you can still savor the small triumphs of today. I recommend that you remind yourself that *today* is a great day.

Are You Feeling Bored?

"I do the same things every day. I'm tired of this school uniform. Nothing exciting ever happens to me."

Everything eventually loses its newness and freshness. Flowers wilt, silver tarnishes, colors fade, paint peels and cracks, white sneakers become gray and worn, socks get holes, pant knees fray, china gets hairline cracks, books come apart and chewing gum loses its flavor and texture. After a while, even our life starts to appear gray. We can't be blamed if we assume, then, that the same thing happens to our minds.

When one's mind loses its freshness and originality, life becomes a circle. One goes round and round but not forward. The days, months and years pass by in a fog of gray, boring sameness. There is a lot of rushing to complete routine tasks, but very little enthusiasm and excitement.

We study, work, spend money, get tired and rest, eat, drink and sleep, and then we do it all over again — day after day. Once in a while we try a new diet. Mostly we are tired — tired of our surroundings, our jobs, and the people we meet each day.

Do we perhaps feel tired of ourselves too?

Is it any wonder that we feel bored? "It has been estimated that 90 percent of the thoughts a person has in a day are a literal repeat of his thoughts of the day before."

We are all busy. Each of us has a variety of responsibilities, talents and hobbies that eat up our time. Yet we all have a common need to nurture our inner selves — our hearts and our minds.

American culture focuses on the exterior — the mind is no big deal. But it is an enormous deal! Just because billions of people walk the earth, it does not in any way diminish the importance of what *you* are thinking and feeling.

We can't change other people's erroneous perceptions. But we can make sure to give our soul every bit of reverence it deserves. We can take time to appreciate and remember that Hashem is our Father and our King. Ultimately what matters most is to honor and celebrate our inner selves.

Notice and Celebrate!

Remember that every day you are a new person. As King David prayed, "Create for me, Hashem, a pure heart, and a pure, honest spirit renew within me" (*Tehillim* 51:12).

Our soul should not age. Our spirit is spiritual and therefore it lasts forever and never becomes weak or dull. Every day brings new opportunities for the joy and enrichment of the healthy mind. Imagine that you put the wrong lens solution on your contact lenses (this really happened) and couldn't see for 24 hours. The joy at regaining your vision is boundless. You would literally sing about the Creator's bounty. Each raindrop, each flower, each star, each cloud is a brand new miracle for you to notice and appreciate. However, in order to take full advantage of your young spirit and be inspired, you have to listen to its voice.

In the following parable from *Sing, You Righteous*, Rav Avigdor Miller shows us the importance of having a good mind. The treasures that life offers us can only be uncovered through awareness:

Imagine that you purchased a vacant lot, erected a house there, and lived there for thirty years. Then one night the telephone rings, and you hear a quavering old voice: "I must inform you that I am the last survivor of a group that buried a chest of gems on the premises where your house now stands. I am about to die, and therefore I wish you to know." Now you are so delirious with joy that you cannot sleep. You are wealthy! But actually for thirty years you were the legal possessor of this unclaimed treasure. What is the factor that makes you happy today instead of thirty years earlier?

It is the knowledge of what we possess. If we are unaware of what we have, or only faintly aware of its true value, we actually do not possess it.

Each of us has many treasures within. However, we keep many of them locked up and don't use them. It is necessary for healthy living that we make the most of our potential by taking on new challenges. However, most of us fear change and push off anything that seems like extra work. We resent ourselves for remaining immobile, while at the same time we can't rally our resources for change. The burden of potential failure caused by our faulty traits weighs on us. We aren't satisfied with ourselves, yet we retain the status quo.

If we knew with certainty that a little work could reveal a wonderful treasure that is lying right in our own backyard, surely we would run out immediately and begin working. Our soul can be rejuvenated every morning. A single decision or experience can change our lives remarkably, as Cheryl's story illustrates.

❧ Decide to Be a New Person

My uncle was in a car accident. His car looked like a crumpled ball of aluminum foil. Afterwards, he was taken to the hospital where he spent three days undergoing a series of serious tests. They checked him from head to toe. When a person is tested for a serious injury or illness, although they think they are fine their imagination tortures them with doubts. While lying in the hospital bed between tests he thought a lot about how fragile life is. He decided that life is too short to carry grudges. What if he really had suddenly left this world without a chance to make peace with all of his family? He spent his free moments between tests calling up everyone in the family and healing his relationships with them. There is one brother he hadn't spoken to for five years with whom he reconciled.

Baruch Hashem, all the tests came back negative and he was fine, except for a broken arm that healed in eight weeks. It might not be right to say this, but I can't help wondering if we would have gained this new family unity if not for the accident.

〜⌖〜

If you invest creative energy in your service of Hashem, your love and inspiration will grow. You will find new strength and hope. If, however, you let your bad traits overpower you, the negative energy will expand. If you remain the same, your periods of inspiration and discouragement will be equal (*Sefer Alei Shur*).

Open Yourself to Growth in Your Life!

Can I renew an old friendship?

Meet someone new or revive a relationship that already exists. Many times we lose contact with people just because we're busy and put off calling for so long that now we feel embarrassed to connect with them again. Most times, friendships can be revived. The same things that caused you to relate well with your friend six years ago are usually there now.

How can I stop procrastinating?

Sometimes the days turn into weeks, simply because we put things off. Make that phone call within 48 hours. Write that letter, and this time mail it. If your friend lives nearby decide that you will meet each other this month. Someone once told me, "When someone says, 'This is an open invitation — come anytime,' it does not feel like they invited me. I still have to call and ask them when I can come and worry that perhaps this particular day isn't good." A real invitation is specific: "Are you busy this Shabbos? We would love to have you join us." So, what are you waiting for?

How can I change the way I communicate?

Do we hear what we are saying? Do we listen to what others are saying? Frequently, things are said quickly and we often don't think about what we have said until after we've said it. We also don't really listen to each other. Even when we don't interrupt, our thoughts aren't focused well on what the other person is saying. Instead, our mind wanders and we are not truly paying attention. Make a concerted effort to change how you communicate — think before you speak and listen attentively to others.

If you have a second language that you speak infrequently try using it more often. I know I should speak Yiddish more, so for one Shabbos I decided to speak exclusively in Yiddish. I found that I said fewer negative things and spoke no *lashon hara* on that Shabbos. Since the unfamiliar language slowed me down a bit I had to think before I spoke.

When was the last time I really noticed the Shabbos candles?

Someone asked R' Shimshon Pincus *zt"l*, "You speak so beautifully about the holiness of Shabbos. However, I don't feel those enthusiastic wondrous emotions you describe. How can I feel the holiness of Shabbos?" R' Pincus asked, "What do you do after you light the Shabbos candles?" The woman replied, "Well, after hurrying to get everything ready for Shabbos I'm so tired. I feel relieved that I finished on time. I light the candles and then go to the couch to lie down. Usually, I fall asleep until my husband comes home." R' Pincus suggested, "Why don't you spend some time sitting by the Shabbos candles and noticing their beauty? The *Shechinah* comes into your home just like it enters every Jewish home, but you won't notice it if you go away from it as soon as it enters."

Light the Shabbos candles early and spend some extra time looking at them and praying near them. When we light the Shabbos candles we invite G-d's presence into our home. It awakens in us the feeling that Hashem is close to us. The *Shechinah* warms our existence. If we don't turn away, we will absorb more holiness.

Have you ever received a Divine "refund"?

Forgive! Sometimes people disappoint us. They may have promised something and then not kept their word. They may have suddenly said something cruel for no reason. We may have used someone as a reference for a camp application and the person we trusted said something critical about us. Yet somehow we do accomplish our goal. Although the person who promised to come doesn't show, someone else surprises us and offers to help. Although the insult hurt, there were other people who did recognize our efforts and appreciate us. Although one reference said something critical the camp director gave us a chance anyway.

Why did things work out anyway? Did it happen by itself? Were we just fortunate? The *Chovos HaLevavos* explains that at times we suffer disappointment, but then Hashem gives us success from an unexpected source. This is Hashem's method of instructing us that everything is in His hands (*Chovos HaLevavos, Shaar Avodas Elokim* 8). Yet even after years have passed we will continue carrying feelings of resentment against those who made life difficult for us. If Hashem issued the "refund" is it right that we should still be angry at the loss? Forgive! When we forgive others it is a mitzvah that brings blessing to the world.

✦ *Visit Your Hero*

Have you ever asked yourself, what experience could I pursue today that would expand my life?

There is no limit to what you can accomplish in life. It starts with imagination — a dream, an ideal which can also broaden your life. Where do we learn those dreams? One way is by taking the time to visit with our heroes, someone who is close to us and is really special. It may be someone who is an unusual success — not with fanfare and publicity but quietly and inconspicuously. In the interview below a teen shares her visit with her hero — her grandmother.

QUESTION: What happened before the War of Independence in Israel?

ANSWER: We saw *hashgachas Hashem* constantly. During World War II, Rommel, a top Nazi commander, was already in Alexandria, Egypt. He announced that he was going to enter Israel. We went to participate in a day of prayer at the grave of the Ohr HaChaim. A great *tzaddik* lay his head on the gravestone. It became very quiet. Then he picked his head up and smiled and said, "Rommel won't come." He was asked how he knew. The *tzaddik* answered that he saw the holy Name of Hashem shining on the tombstone, which was a sign of mercy. A while later we all watched as the planes that had been heading toward Jerusalem fell into the Mediterranean Sea.

QUESTION: What were some other trials that you experienced?

ANSWER: Your great-grandfather Dovid was in America looking for a job. Because of the war he could not return to Jerusalem. I was alone in Jerusalem caring for our six children. We had no telephone. We wrote to each other once a week. When war broke out even those letters couldn't be delivered.

I gave birth to my seventh child alone. I had no husband to depend on or consult with. How does one make a *bris* in the middle of the war? We were sitting in the shelter on the day of the *bris*. Who would bring a *mohel?* I had begged the hospital to allow me to stay and make a *bris* there. That day there was a cease-fire for 2 hours. There was a lull without bombs falling. Everyone was free to leave the shelters. My relatives came to the *bris*. Your great-grandfather was there. He gave the baby the name Zev. I wanted to add the name Yisrael because he was born in Eretz Yisrael at a dangerous time.

QUESTION: What did you do right after the war?

ANSWER: I promised G-d that if the whole family came out of the war alive I would take them to Miron. After the war I hailed the first truck I saw. It happened to be a flatbed truck. My seven young sons and I boarded. There were a lot of people on the truck but they were all military people. They tried to convince me to postpone my trip but I was determined to fulfill my promise at the first possible moment. I ignored the warnings of danger. In great discomfort we went on to Miron.

Chayala F.

Chapter 8

The Gift of Appreciation

• Perspective

• Knowledge

Lessons From School

Sometimes people are inspired very quickly but get uninspired even quicker. Our goal is to learn how to stay inspired even after a long time.

(Mimi Shwartz)

◆ *School: A Different Perspective*

*H*ow is it that someone like me — a person who used to fall asleep in school — is actually feeling excited about going to school?

I'll bet I can make you laugh. I will simply ask you one question: "Is school your favorite place to be?"

You wake up too early and you never feel quite ready. You run out in the morning with your coat open and a nervous stomach. You get there just a minute before the bell rings. There are some teachers you enjoy and some lessons you look forward to, but there are too many tests. Sometimes there are two tests a day, but one teacher called it a quiz so that she could legally squeeze it in. However, you know it wasn't a quiz, because it had fifty fill-ins and a map of Africa. You look at your watch at least fifty times a day.

There is never a break. During recess you have to catch up on homework. During lunch you are reviewing the questions in algebra with a friend who is a whiz at math. Between periods all you have is 5 minutes, but often your teacher continues past the bell. There is never a chance to catch your breath.

Even when you are sick you go to school, because you know that if you stay home there will be too much work to make up. Your shoes are dusty and your navy skirt has white patches of chalk dust. There is even chalk dust in your nose. For 8 hours you wait for the bell to ring. These endless bells make your teeth hurt. At last, the final bell rings. You feel light and free walking home. On Wednesday afternoon you tell yourself, "Hmm ... only one and a half days to Shabbos."

You are standing at your doorway. You ring the bell and smile to yourself. You can't wait to come in and sit down. Everywhere across the nation mothers will greet daughters with the same question as soon as they open the door. "How was school?" You shrug your shoulders and say, "Okay."

Sometimes we learn to appreciate that which we previously took for granted when it is shown to us from a different perspective. Liza is a 13-year-old girl who recently arrived from Russia. One night I was talking to her on the phone and I casually asked, "How was your day in school?" In her newly acquired hesitant English she told me, "Shaindy, I am so happy. This is the first time I go to yeshivah. I am so happy. There are only Jewish people around me!"

At that moment I realized that my monotonous ordinary days of school are a gift. Did I ever think of being happy that there are only Jewish people around me? Did I ever realize how lucky I was to be able to learn about our traditions since the very first day of nursery? Did I realize how grateful I must be that I can say blessings and prayers without worry or fear? Did I realize that Judaism was served to me on a silver platter? Did I know that not everyone is so blessed?

Shaindy S.

❧

Mrs. S. grew up in Lugano, Switzerland. It is a town with a very small Jewish community.

QUESTION: Why did your family live in Lugano ?

MRS. S.: My parents moved to Lugano before World War II. After the war, we were already settled in Lugano. We had cousins there. My father had established a business. It would have been difficult to move.

QUESTION: In what ways were things more difficult because of where you lived?

MRS. S.: Many basic things that we take for granted when we live in New York required a great deal of effort. Keeping a kosher home took planning and hard work. If we didn't have supper one night we couldn't order take-out food. We didn't have take-out stores. We baked our own challah and cake. Grocery items were limited. There was just one small kosher grocery that sold very few items at an expensive price. Meat and chicken were imported because the Swiss government didn't permit *shechitah*. They cost a fortune. It was difficult to find appropriate clothing in local stores. Therefore our clothes were made to order or we did our own sewing.

QUESTION: What was your social life like?

MRS. S.: I had very few Jewish friends, and I didn't have even one friend who was my age. I went to public school because there was no Jewish school. I didn't have close school friends. Some of the girls were cordial, but they treated me differently. I saw the other Jewish girls once a week in shul.

QUESTION: How were things different in school?

MRS. S.: The teachers were anti-Semitic. You felt it even though they tried to conceal it. They did not show it outright but it was obvious. Some of the girls would even tell me that I'm dirty because I'm a Jew and all Jews are dirty.

QUESTION: Did you have trouble on Shabbos or Yom Tov?

MRS. S.: Yes, when my mother went to school she had to attend on Shabbos. She didn't write or carry her briefcase to school, but she had to be there. When I went to school, we already had permission to stay home. When I went back on Monday the first thing the teacher would do was check my notebooks to see if I had made up my work. I always had to attend school on Chol HaMoed and even on Hoshana Rabbah. On Chanukah, I worried about being home in time because I couldn't ask to leave early.

QUESTION: What major change did you feel when you moved to America?

MRS. S.: It is so good to live among so many Jewish people in one place. I still love to look out the window every morning and see hundreds of yellow buses taking little Jewish children to yeshivah. I wish that just one or two of these buses could have been in Lugano when I grew up.

QUESTION: What message would you like to share?

MRS. S.: I wish that children would learn not to take their blessings for granted. Appreciate the fact that you can go to a Jewish school. You feel at home and at ease. The girls don't stare at you because you have Jewish friends. You have Jewish teachers. Every day you should think *ashreinu, ma tov chelkeinu,* how fortunate are we, how good is our portion. Appreciate every *frum* Jew you see when you walk down the street. Care about each other and be friendly to one another. You are very fortunate.

❧ Another Ordinary Day

Today was an ordinary day. I woke up this morning, couldn't find my shoes, skipped breakfast and rushed to school, barging through the doors at 9:01. My day began in a typical way. I sat through classes and breaks as usual. Baruch Hashem. Just a week ago it wasn't like this and tomorrow things may be different. We are living in times when there is nothing that can be predicted. We are surrounded by fear so thick it is tangible. We are left solely in the protection of Hashem. We exist only because of Divine mercy.

Several months ago, toward the end of Shabbos, I was visiting my neighbor. Suddenly, we were surprised to see five police cars racing down the road with sirens blaring. Following them were a police bus, police van, police station wagon, police tow-truck and a fleet of police motorcycles. I do not live in the best neighborhood, in fact, the community has many Arab residents. My sister counted twenty-seven police vehicles speeding by. They filled our street and the surrounding blocks with wailing sirens, whirring lights and wary officers. We were certain that the entire precinct must have emptied and come to our block. Why? I decided to leave my friend's house and proceed homeward.

As I headed down the block, a burly police officer barred my path. Holding out his calloused palm he demanded, "What are you doing here?" It reminded me of incidents I had read about in Nazi Germany and the perpetual, "Halt, who goes there?" Timidly, I replied, "I live here."

"You do? Let me escort you." At my door, in a voice that sent shivers up my spine, he issued a final command, "Stay indoors."

We watched the police evacuate the building to our left. A crowd of puzzled people huddled in a group on the sidewalk and waited nervously for the police to take them to a safer place. What was going on? We didn't have a clue. Squads of police officers on foot and masses of vehicles went up and down the street until the wee hours of the morning. Finally, they found a 60-year-old terrorist who had planted a bomb in downtown Brooklyn. This madman was living in the apartment building right near my house! His apartment was full of explosives. When the police finally caught him, we all pulled down the shades and sighed with relief. The entire precinct sped off as the first light of dawn appeared.

This occurred before the World Trade Center tragedy — before the incredible carnage that rocked the world. This was before we discovered that a man who lived just a few houses down from us was actually one of the hijackers. He was the quiet type, highly respectable and a pilot by profession. Another hijacker lived in my grandparents' vicinity. Only two weeks after the World Trade Center collapse, the Arabs across the street were arrested. On my street, the police are outside the mosque. Inside, beady-eyed, sinister men beat upon bongo drums with hatred in their eyes.

However, today was an ordinary day. Today, I came home safely. The night was quiet. All I can say is, "Thank You, Hashem, for giving and sustaining life. Thank You, Hashem, for protecting me, because my neighbors are capable of blowing up the area."

Miriam Brocho Minzter

✦

We should not become stuck in our routine. If we remember to appreciate the ordinary things and every day of calm and peace we will feel inspired.

Don't take life for granted.

Thank Hashem for another ordinary day.

As you pull up the covers before you fall asleep visualize Hashem covering you with a blanket of His loving protection.

✦ *Packing My Knapsack*

I remember packing my briefcase for the first day of school. Acquiring school supplies was fun. Sometimes I went to more than one store. These were easy decisions. I smiled when I chose a favorite pen, a pretty folder and the perfect loose-leaf. My friend had a marvelous idea — we would decorate our loose-leafs. We bought clear contact paper and a simple canvas loose-leaf. Then we chose our favorite summer photographs and arranged them in a collage on the front and back, using tape to keep everything in place. Finally, we covered the entire loose-leaf with clear contact paper. I wanted everything to be exactly right.

I enjoyed preparing my clothes too. We had a uniform, but we still had some choice in what to wear. Everyone didn't have the exact same navy blue skirt or the exact style light-blue blouse. I had fun choosing these things and looked forward to wearing something new.

Preparing for a new beginning was exciting. I thought about the year that knapsacks for school were first intro-duced. I smiled when I remembered my first set of magic markers. I received them on my birthday. They really did seem like a magical writing instrument when they first appeared on the toy-store shelf. Most of my friends didn't have them yet. As I put my new loose-leaf, new folders and new notebooks into my knapsack I had many plans.

I thought about the friends I hadn't seen during the summer. I was going to see them soon. Would I like my seat? Which teachers would I have? New notebooks still give me a hopeful, glowing feeling that is hard to describe. This was a new start and I could leave last year's flaws behind. I resolved that this year I wouldn't procrastinate. I would review each night and keep my notes organized.

Of course I worried. I prayed for success in every detail. I understood the meaning of the words in bentching — "May we find charm and kind understanding in the eyes of Hashem and man." I yearned for acceptance and approval from my friends and teachers.

As I packed my knapsack, I made an important decision. I had spent the summer in Eretz Yisrael. It was exciting to walk in the same places that the greatest people in history walked. I went on a Tanach tour and the pages of the Navi became real for me. I walked on the mountain where Shmuel HaNavi had lived, taught and shared his prophecy with hundreds of students. I *said a berachah — "Thank You, Hashem, for making miracles for my forefathers at this place in Givon." Our tour guide retold the story of Yehoshua stopping the sun in Givon. It visit to Eretz Yisrael helped me realize that Torah study was not just another subject. It was a study that was a part of me. It was important and I cared about it.*

I decided to purchase a fabric-covered journal. This would be my special place for recording the lessons I wanted to cherish. I resolved that each day I'd make a note of something meaningful I had learned that day. When a teacher shared a significant story, I wrote that in my journal. If we had a guest speaker I took the journal to school and wrote my notes in there. When I went to the Bais Yaakov convention I took the journal along. Reminders and mementos of special days were saved and taped in too.

Several weeks ago I reminisced about packing my knapsack on the first day of school so many years ago. I was listening to a lecture on tape. The speaker described keeping a special notebook for Jewish history. Rabbi Rottenberg's classes inspired her to become a teacher of Jewish history herself. She declared that she still has her notebook decades later. I smiled because Rabbi Rottenberg was my teacher too. I recalled coming home and copying Rabbi Rottenberg's lectures into my journal. I still have my notebook, too.

Candy Bags

Candy bags are usually given out at least once a week in first grade. When she was in the ninth grade my daughter came home looking glum and exclaimed, "In first grade we learned about the *Parashah* every week. When *Bereishis* was finished we had a party; now our teacher announced a final!" You may have mixed emotions about finishing the term when you will be facing a final instead of a party. Why not prepare candy bags for your class so that you can celebrate a *siyum*? This could be a great new tradition to start at your school.

∽✌

We often don't realize the value of the things that are lying around in corners. It could be that at the time we were busy with something else and therefore this treasure was ignored. It could be that it wasn't important then but now it is. Now we understand things differently.

I'm always saving things in case I might need them. Usually this isn't a good idea, it leads to a cluttered life. But in the area of knowledge I've never regretted it. I am so happy that I have twenty-year-old notebooks and journals from my school years. I have several tapes of my favorite teachers that I listen to again and again. Somehow I learn a new lesson every time. These are things from which you might gain new insight. I didn't save my math book, and my economics book is obsolete, but the Torah lessons are of a different category.

When can I sit down and look at these old notebooks? Perhaps Friday night is an opportune time. After I light the candles I can sit and read a Torah thought and reflect on the lessons I value most. I can think about the past week and ask myself how I can put these ideals into practice. I can gather those pearls of good feelings I hadn't stopped to notice before.

I can think about the feeling of discovery. Unearthing a nugget of knowledge is a pleasant revelation. It's hard for me to decide if it's more fun to buy something new or to discover the value of something I already have.

Lessons From the Classroom

● A New World Created Every Day

by Helen Keller

The world I see with my fingers is alive, ruddy and satisfying. Touch brings the blind many sweet certainties, which our more for-

tunate fellows miss, because their sense of touch is uncultivated. When they look at things, they put their hands in their pockets.

Through the sense of touch I know the faces of friends, the illimitable variety of straight and curved lines, all surfaces, the exuberance of the soil, the delicate shapes of flowers, the notable forms of trees, and the range of mighty winds.

The senses assist and reinforce each other to such an extent that I am not sure whether touch or smell tells me the most about the world. Everywhere there is the river of touch joined by the brooks of odor perception. Each season has its distinctive odors. The spring is earthy and full of sap. July is rich with the odor of ripening grain and hay. As the season advances, a crisp, dry, mature odor predominates, and goldenrod, tansy and everlasting mark the onward march of the year. In autumn, soft, alluring scents fill the air, floating from thicket, grass, flower, and tree, and they tell me of time and change, of death and life's renewal, desire and its fulfillment.

After my education began, the world which came within my reach was all alive. I spelled to my blocks and my dogs.

Without imagination what a poor thing my world would be! My garden would be a silent patch of earth strewn with sticks of a variety of shapes and smells. But when the eye of my mind is opened to its beauty, the bare ground brightens beneath my feet, and the hedge-row bursts into leaf, and the rose-tree shakes its fragrance everywhere.

Necessity gives to the eye a precious power of seeing, and in the same way it gives a precious power of feeling to the whole body. The silence and darkness, which are said to shut me in, open my door most hospitably to countless sensations that inform, admonish and amuse. With my three trusty guides, touch, smell and taste, I make many excursions into the borderland of experience which is in sight of the city of light.

Our blindness changes not a whit the course of inner realities. Of us it is true as it is of the seeing that the most beautiful world is always entered through the imagination. If you wish to be something you are not — something fine, noble, good — you shut your eyes, and for one dreamy moment you are that which you long to be.

The Teacher

When my heart feels weary
And my thoughts are gray,
When clouds of worry gather
I search
For words to warm my heart,
To quench my thirst,
To help me find
Peace of mind.

I grasp a glistening memory
From a distant time and place;
I squeeze my eyes shut to see
A smiling, glowing face
The teacher helped me,
She opened the door—
Her lessons and her actions
Showed me I can do much more,

Now I stand on the other side,
I'm in front of the desk.
Before so many searching eyes
My lessons are prepared, but am I ready?
A child with many questions
Looks up to me,
I'm supposed to be a role model
Eloquent with clues.

Once again I grasp a glistening memory
Of a smiling glowing face.
Now that I'm the teacher,
I'm in this important place.
I pray for wisdom
To open new doors—
With lessons and actions
I'll show those who look toward me
That they can do much more.

Be an answer to someone's prayer today.

(C. Y. Brown)

Thank You to a Teacher

Teachers don't expect students to say how they really feel. They don't anticipate a thank-you note at the end of the year (although it would be thoughtful). Students may have gained a lot from a teacher yet they feel timid and reticent to express it, especially if their peers will know. For a teenage girl to openly say that she admires her teacher and has gained a lot from her takes a great deal of courage. Perhaps now that she has written a note of appreciation it will pave the way and others will do it too.

My tenth-grade teacher was Rebbetzin Weintraub. She's an amazing person. Rebbetzin Weintraub was like a grand-mother to all of us. She always shared a smile with the class. Rebbetzin W. invited us to her home for class parties that were filled with lessons that came straight from her heart. She treated us with an unbelievable amount of caring and respect. She dealt with all of us equally and made each person feel special. Rebbetzin Weintraub wasn't one of those teachers who liked a girl better because of her marks. Instead she liked us for who we were. She truly loved us all and knew how to show it. I learned many things from her that I will always remember. Thank you, Rebbetzin Weintraub.

B.S.

The Gift
of Giving

Find Your Sparkle

In life we are given gifts from Above. These gifts are tools for growth, an important purpose of life. We are responsible for channeling our talents in the right direction. This, however, is more easily said than done. Many people go through life without once acknowledging that their talents are a gift from Above. The gift of giving can be channeled in many ways.

A respected individual in our community is blessed with the talent of persuasion. She can persuade people to do just about anything, and she does it quite easily. When she was a young girl, a friend once jokingly commented to her that she should become a salesperson when she grows up. This friend painted a glowing picture of how successful she might be in sales and how it could open up many opportunities for her.

The years passed and this individual became a teacher. She spoke from her heart, piercing through walls of resistance and reaching her students' hearts. She generated enthusiasm and helped teenagers overcome their struggles and doubts. Many loyal students declared that they owed their lives to her.

Recently the teacher met her old friend. "I followed your suggestion," she said. The friend was ecstatic. Then the teacher added, "I became a salesperson for knowledge. I sell knowledge and my students acquire it. I'm a teacher."

No one would have blamed this woman had she joined a car dealership or other enterprise and amassed a fortune. Yet she decided to devote her talents to a higher cause. Each of us has a talent that is waiting to shine. We have to find the right way to bring it forth.

Nechoma and Shira S.

Questions

At the end of each day ask yourself questions that will help you become a better person and accomplish more.

(*Begin Again Now*, Rabbi Z. Pliskin)

Some questions that you might ask yourself to help you become a better person and accomplish more:

1. What were my greatest moments today?
2. How did I give to others today?
3. What hopeful idea do I want to remember before I go to sleep?
4. What did I learn today?

The first time you read these questions your mind may draw a blank. Don't be discouraged if answers don't materialize in an instant. These questions are powerful tools to help you overcome feelings of inadequacy, insecurity, irritability and agitation. We tend to focus on the conflicts, delays and obstacles in our lives. These four questions turn our attention to the positive. They help us feel certain, hopeful and confident by focusing our attention on the good things that are happening in our lives now.

What were my greatest moments today?

We have to strive to take hold of our greatest daily moments and save them so that they won't be lost forever. The secret of true wealth is in our attitude. If we feel fortunate and blessed we are wealthy, as our Sages have said, "Who is wealthy? The one who is happy with what he has" (*Avos* 4:1).

In the Priestly Blessing we say, "May Hashem bless you and watch over you." Rebbetzin Feige Twerski of Milwaukee explained this as follows: May Hashem bless you and watch that you continue to feel always that you are blessed. It is human nature that we enjoy our blessings when they are fresh, but after a while we become accustomed to them and take them for granted.

What were your greatest moments today? Did someone give you a compliment? Were you successful in avoiding gossip for a 2-hour period? Did you finally keep a promise that was long neglected? Did your child's first tooth sprout? Did you try a new recipe and everyone liked the results? Catch those moments. Look at them, appreciate and savor them. Your experiences can be a true learning resource.

When you acknowledge your moments of success it helps you look at other people with kindness. It helps you look at yourself with a gentle eye as well. This brings about greater joy and reminds you to smile. Self-awareness can stimulate energy, and lead to a blossoming of your spiritual abilities. You remember your soul.

Another benefit of savoring our small joys is that it motivates us to accomplish more in our lives. The saying might have been, "If at first you do succeed you will try again." The only way to feel successful is if one learns to enjoy the learning process rather than wait for perfection before smiling in one's mind.

A small success brings a larger success. Do one bite-size part of the overwhelming task that you have to face. The success will give you peace of mind.

How did I give to others today?

There are many simple things we can give to others. While accomplishing routine tasks we can seize the opportunity to warm someone's heart. Daily encounters can become meaningful when we tune in to the feelings of the many people we pass in the corridors of life every day.

What if we greeted someone we didn't know well in a manner that conveyed that we were really glad to see them?

Would buying something for a classmate when we are at the grocery during our lunch recess break the ice and start a meaningful friendship?

Wouldn't it be thoughtful to take notes for someone who is absent and send them to her house with a cheerful greeting?

How would our teacher's day change if we mustered our courage and went up to her desk to thank her for an inspiring lesson?

❧ *Cupcake*

*O*ne day in eleventh grade I sat at my desk in the classroom eating lunch with my friends. We sat in groups of two or three girls and talked quietly as we munched on our tuna sandwiches.

The door opened and in unison we jumped out of our seats and crowded around our classmate's desk.

"Surprise!" we shouted. A huge birthday card was extracted from the pink and white striped bag and placed on the desk. Everyone in the class had secretly signed the card earlier that morning. "Happy Birthday!" we all shouted.

The door opened again. Our friend looked up. Three girls entered holding a single cupcake aloft. It was the biggest chocolate cupcake I had ever seen. The top was covered with black and white frosting. One single tiny candle burned in the center. Our group began singing, "Happy Birthday" with exuberance.

The birthday girl gratefully accepted the cupcake, smiling shyly. Before she could say a word, a mixture of surprise, delight and gratitude welled up in her eyes. Finally our singing ended. "Thank you for remembering my birthday," she whispered.

I glanced at my classmate several times that afternoon — she was radiant with joy.

☙❧

As soon as a guest comes to your house, give him refreshments. When the angels came to Avraham, he said, "I will fetch a piece of bread that you may refresh your hearts" (*Bereishis* 18:5). R' Yisrael Salanter points out that although Avraham planned to serve an entire meal, he offered them some bread, which would satisfy their hunger until he would be able to prepare their meal. This type of snack helps a person calm down and feel refreshed, as the verse says — "that you may refresh your hearts."

There are many opportunities to show hospitality to guests. We can also extend this principle to our families. It is sometimes hard to have food on the table at the exact moment that our families arrive home. Yet we can have a salad, or some fruit or some other nutritious (or semi-nutritious) snack ready for them so they can refresh themselves. We learn from Avraham that this light snack is not just a courtesy. When someone enters our home tired and hungry, a snack can help calm his heart.

Birthday Bags

Spend an afternoon personalizing a birthday bag for someone you know. Fill the birthday bag with treats like stickers, stationery, earrings, a cassette tape or any other gift you know your friend will appreciate. Hand deliver it to your friend on her special day. Your friend will enjoy looking at this cheerful bag that's covered with small pictures and the signatures of her friends.

You will need:

White canvas bag (available in art supply stores)

Permanent markers

Ribbons and felt pieces to glue onto the bag

Colored glue or glitter glue

Patterns to trace

What hopeful idea do I want to remember before I go to sleep?

Each day offers us its gifts. However, we may have problems, doubts and worries to deal with at the same time. What will we focus on? Is our cup half full or is it half empty? What thoughts could make us feel more hopeful? Perhaps looking at photographs of all the people we love or wonderful places we've visited; perhaps indulging in the pleasure of a long-distance phone call to an upbeat friend who lives out of town. Maybe investing in a beautifully bound *sefer Tehillim* that we will want to open every day, or wearing "special occasion" jewelry that we received as a gift from someone we admire will raise our spirits. Each day offers us the gift of being a special occasion.

Sometimes giving to others sustains our feelings of hope. A participant at the *Tehillim* lecture told me the following about remaining hopeful:

"My friend's mother is an elderly woman who is going through chemotherapy. She doesn't seem like someone you'd expect this from, but she is always cheerful. Last year her hobby was baking and decorating cakes. All the time it was cakes, cakes, cakes. Her daughter said, 'Ma, you are baking more than we can eat.' This year she's knitting. She's learning new patterns and adding her original touch. She's knitting sweaters for everyone in the family. I asked her, 'How do you go through with it? How do you handle it?' It's obvious that the doctors think she has no future, yet she ignores them and is not only surviving but living vibrantly. She fills her days with creative acts of giving to others. She told me, 'You have to live with hope. Without hope, you cannot live.'

"When I'm worried and can't sleep, I just picture myself walking into her house, sitting down next to her and letting her take my hand in hers. I tell her my worries and she smiles and tells me, 'You have to live with hope. Without hope you cannot live.' It works. I fall asleep."

What did I learn today?

The first day of school stirs up mixed feelings in us. We feel hopeful yet apprehensive, eager yet anxious, optimistic but worried on that important day. Behind an assured smile there hides a tense heart. Sometimes we are ready to put our best effort into our work, yet we wonder if the teacher will take a moment to notice.

Your school years are an opportunity. They can be the best years of your life. You will meet many people as you pass through the grades. If you are seriously determined to expand your horizons, Hashem will surely send you the opportunity to learn and grow. Someone you encounter may make a dramatic difference in your life. A teacher may convince you that you have greatness within you. A friend may give you a glimpse of who you really are, of your specialness, and then the world will never be the same again.

A best-selling author said that when he was young, his father asked him every night, "What have you learned today?" The boy knew he had to have an answer — and a good one. If he hadn't learned anything interesting in school that day, he'd scurry to the bookshelves in his home. Decades later, this man still won't go to bed until he's learned something new and valuable for the day.

You don't learn only from books. You can learn from your experiences. You can learn from the people you meet. You can even learn while you are doing something else by listening to a tape of a lecture.

❧ *Giving Hope*

Sima teaches a nursery class. She's about 5'7" tall. Her blonde wig just touches her shoulders. She has rosy cheeks and a glowing smile. There are no wings sprouting from her shoulders. If you walked down the avenue you'd pass her without a second glance, but her former students will run half a block to greet her. She is one of those teachers a student will always remember. When they think of her they smile.

A 3-year-old girl thinks that Morah Sima is the most wonderful person in the universe. She can do so many things. She sings and draws and even plays the keyboard. Imagine — if you sing a song for her twice she can play it back for you even though she's never heard that song before. However, she has another talent that surpasses that one. She uses her moments well.

Every day has 1440 minutes. Somehow, it always feels like we need at least 500 more of them. There is always so much to do. Your responsibilities feel overwhelming. You are always in a hurry and always behind and always catching up. How many of those moments do you use productively to connect with another individual and give him or her a spark of hope? Typically, you pass dozens of people every day without really seeing them. You are so busy that you fail to pause to nurture a relationship. Perhaps you are busy sorting out your own problems. You care and you want to reach out, but at the moment you are distracted.

If efficiency is your priority then you may just be too preoccupied to notice a lonely soul. Do you hear the sounds of silence, the hearts that cry without words? A girl is sitting near you, alone. She is looking your way and trying to get the courage to walk over. Perhaps she offered you a pen and hoped you'd begin a conversation. You just mumbled a thank you and hurried away. How would your life be different if you had put things on pause and taken a moment to connect?

It only takes a moment to give someone hope. Sima's goal in her classroom is to say as many kind expressions as possible. She observes each individual that she passes with a sense of understanding. She tries to notice something they did right. It may not be something fascinating, but since she wants to help she'll make a fuss about it anyway. She might invite that person to sit near her. It doesn't even take 60 seconds to say, "I'm happy to see you," or "Have a successful day."

A 3-year-old is often a very lonely individual who really wants her mother's consoling embrace. This new student had to get up too early and she doesn't know if her shoes are on the right feet. She ate breakfast quickly with her eyes half closed. She cried at the bus stop but she had to go anyhow. Now she's in school. She feels cold, but she can't find her sweater. She feels thirsty, but she's too shy to ask for a drink. She has to go to the bathroom, but she's definitely too embarrassed to mention it. Everything is new and she feels alone and confused.

Sima teaches twenty-five 3-year-old girls. Sima is not an average teacher, because although there are so many girls each one is treated as her child. She touches every individual because she has a good word for each one. Each child needs help with something. Some need help putting on their coats, while others need help getting their food on their spoons. There are those who need help cutting shapes or holding crayons. Some need help in joining a game while others need help in cooperating and sharing. In 10 minutes there may be three crises. Nevertheless, although Sima is very busy she still takes time to notice and care. It only takes a moment to give someone hope.

One little girl seemed scared and alone. As the days turned to weeks she continued to sit silently in the back of the room. The toys didn't interest her. She didn't play and she didn't sing. This girl literally said just one word over the course of an entire day. When the teacher called her name as she took attendance this little girl whispered, "Here."

Each day, Sima took a moment to give her hope. She showed her warmth and love. During snack time she invited this lonely girl to sit near her. Every day Sima found things about this girl that she admired. She wasn't embarrassed to applaud this silent girl's effort even if she was the only one clapping. When her student was even a bit helpful Sima complimented her generously. Every day Sima smiled and cheerfully wished this small individual a nice day. Despite everything, Sima didn't see any progress. It's hard to persevere when one's gestures are met with silence, but Sima kept hoping it would make a difference.

The weeks turned to months. Three months into the school year Sima saw a miracle. Suddenly, on a Tuesday, Sima's silent student eagerly approached and asked, "Why is Rochel wearing a hairband and a ponytail? Why doesn't she wear just one of them?" Sima wanted to cry. This was an unbelievable moment. Perhaps all the energy and non-stop encouragement had made a difference after all. These were the first words her student had spoken in three months and she had said two complete sentences. However, Sima pretended that this was the most natural conversation. In a matter-of-fact tone, Morah Sima said, "That's a good question. If you'd like we can both go over and ask Rochel about it."

They did just that. A conversation began between two 3-year-old girls. Now a lonely, silent girl had a friend. An unhappy girl had found her place. One success led to another. This child continued to take risks. A shy little girl asked a question. A shy little girl requested her fair turn. A shy little girl laughed and clapped her hands. A shy little girl ran and grabbed a partner. She began connecting with her classmates, until she chattered happily and participated in the games and sang with enthusiasm. It only takes a moment to give someone hope, and Morah Sima invests many moments in her students' lives.

I remember a friend saying in a class, "If I had a quarter for every time the back door was unlocked and nothing happened, I'd be a wealthy woman." I nodded and thought of those times that I stepped into the street and a car barely avoided hitting me. Basy told me, "The other day a car missed me by inches. I took out my checkbook and immediately wrote out a check to *tzedakah* for $18. If you don't pause to thank Hashem for the miracle right away, you may overlook its significance by the end of the day."

Miracles are everywhere. Just take one baby step and open your mind to see them. Some miracles are obvious; others are more hidden. There is always a message, but you have to want to hear it. Noticing the miracle gives us courage and helps us to grow spiritually. "To the extent that we become enthusiastic with images of Hashem's greatness we will also be filled with happiness because we realize that every aspect of Hashem's greatness is here to benefit us" (R' Shimshon Pincus). If happiness is your goal then pause and identify everyday miracles.

When we feel like throwing in the towel, the ordinary miracles that occur each day can give us strength and energy. We are reminded that everything does not depend on our efforts alone. Hashem is always right by our side. This thought should fill us with awe. However, these ordinary miracles can only be a source of power if we stop, look and notice. *You* have to light the flame in your heart.

《ೲ෴》

People tend to think that only amazing incidents are miracles. Yet every day that we are safe is a miracle. When one hour passes smoothly that is a miracle, too.

One pleasant summer evening, my friend and I decided to take a walk on a country road. As we strolled down the long circular route, we had no idea that an adventure would soon occur. We had started out quite late in the day. We did not take note of the passing time. Suddenly we looked up and saw the familiar streaks of purple and pink filling the sky. The sun was about to set. At first we gazed at the panorama surrounding us and tried to breathe in the mesmerizing beauty. Then it occurred to us that in less than 10 minutes it would turn dark.

There was no point in turning back. The route was a circle and turning back or continuing home would take the same amount of time. We were panic-stricken. It was difficult to walk at a quicker pace because we were afraid of falling. The country road was dark and quiet with no lighting except for occasional passing cars. Although we felt tired, we tried to speed up our walking. Now it was dark and we still had a long way to go.

Suddenly, a light-colored van came to a screeching halt in front of us. We panicked. Terrifying thoughts crossed our minds. As we approached, the van's door opened. A kind-looking woman sat in the van. She appeared pale and upset. Her hands were shaking and in a squeaky voice she explained that she had almost hit us. The road was very dark and narrow and we were wearing dark clothing. The woman had not seen us at all. By some miracle, she managed to stop before the unthinkable happened. After she calmed down she drove us back to our colony.

Miracles happen daily and we must recognize them and appreciate them. My friend and I resolved to be more careful. All of us should endeavor to lead our lives in a way that we won't need to depend on miracles.

Menucha S.

⤳⤲

If we would be aware of the miracles that happen around us every single day, we would see and experience every occurrence from an entirely new perspective. Each person has his or her own way of staying connected to this idea. Some people write things down, while others may want to create a scrapbook of pictures, or share their experiences with someone to whom they feel close. By simply being receptive and aware we can begin to live a deeper and richer life.

If I can't find that important item I don't have to feel upset. It's a setback but I don't have to have an inner tantrum. The struggle to cope needn't make me feel tired. Complaining won't help me find what is missing. Instead of looking at what I don't have and feeling helpless, I can remember that I have options.

I can choose to thank Hashem. I can choose to try again. I can forge ahead. When I adopt a healthy attitude, I will stop looking at the obstacles. This problem feels overwhelming, but I can see beyond it.

I may not be perfect, but I can be really good. I may not be immaculate, but I can still be neat. I may not make everyone happy, but I can make most people happy. I may not be an expert, but I know more today than I knew yesterday. Perhaps I'll find this item that I misplaced soon. In the meantime, I can think about the story of the car keys.

There are situations in my family background that can be considered nothing short of miraculous. This is especially true of experiences that my grandparents had in Nazi concentration camps. Yet my parents have taught me that every second of life is full of miracles. One such hidden "everyday" miracle occurred to my mother about three years ago.

My mother does acts of kindness on a regular basis, especially in using her car. She gives lifts to as many people as possible. Even if their destination is in the opposite direction, she'll offer a lift with a smile. To make her passengers feel at ease she engages them in pleasant conversation. It has also been her preference to walk or drive my sisters and me to or from school until we reach the older grades. I appreciate this special time we have together.

One spring morning my mother entered the house after driving a carload of people to school. Once home, she usually places her keys in a certain section of her handbag so that they will be ready for the afternoon trip. She put her hand in the pocket of her jacket but the keys were not there. Instead, her fingers poked through a hole in that pocket. There was no identification attached to the keys.

My mother left the house and retraced her steps to the car. It was parked two blocks away. She walked back and forth between the car and the house three times, but did not find the keys. During the second time, a neighbor, Mrs. G., was taking out her trash. She asked my mother what the problem was. This neighbor accompanied my mother on her third tip to the car. Then she mentioned that her son would type and print a sign describing the lost keys. My mother thanked her and went home. She felt badly about the incident but she was sure that Hashem was watching.

That afternoon, my mother walked the seventeen blocks to pick up my younger sister. For the next two days, she used my father's keys to drive. Mrs. G. hadn't brought over any signs. My mother assumed that her son hadn't been able to make them after all. Then on the third evening someone called and told us that the keys were hanging on the synagogue's bulletin board around the corner from our home. My mother ran over there and found them.

Of course, she wanted to thank someone. Since the caller had kept his identity secret she couldn't thank him. She went to Mrs. G. to share the good news. My mother found out that Mrs. G.'s son did print the signs. This kind neighbor hadn't wanted to bother us, so she walked around the neighborhood and hung up the signs in the synagogue and on corner poles.

My mother feels that this occurrence isn't just a simple case of lost and found. A miracle occurred in the merit of the kindnesses she performs with her car.

Yehudis R.

❧

*Y*ou may think it's ordinary that the human heart keeps pumping without stopping day after day. Second after second it keeps us alive. Yet we overlook the fact that without that one muscle pumping every second our body could not function. This is not ordinary, it's a miracle.

The human brain can remember an infinite amount of facts each day and it carries them over from day to day. Is it only when an elderly person loses his memory that we appreciate what a gift memory is? Memory is a miracle worthy of thanks.

Adina B.

❧

*W*hen was the last time you realized you were breathing? Our lungs help us breathe in and out many times each minute. We don't feel or think about the experience. Our breathing is peaceful and dependable. It is always there. The air goes in and out thousands of times a day. We aren't sensitive to the miracle of each breath. It just is. However, there are some people who will never take their lungs for granted.

My brother Mendy was a premature baby. He was a tiny four pounds at birth. His lungs weren't developed. He was a child with an uncertain future, an infant with dangers looming over him.

Now our Mendy is, baruch Hashem, a perfectly fine, adorable 2 year old. I learned to be grateful and appreciative when everything is fine. A baby is born so often that we start taking this miracle for granted. In reality, so much can go wrong. We should appreciate everything that goes right. We have to learn to be happy when nothing out of the ordinary occurs.

Tzeena W.

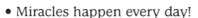

*M*y sister is 2½ years old. When she was about one she fell and banged her head on the ceramic floor. I was very worried. To my great relief when I picked her up I saw that baruch Hashem all she had was a small red bruise on her head. I put a pack of ice on it. I'm thankful that she didn't end up in the hospital. Sometimes I think that angels are assigned to watch toddlers and protect them.

Rochel B.

- Miracles happen every day!
- Every new stage a baby reaches is a miracle.
- When you had a minor illness and recovered it's a miracle.

The Best Insurance

Insurance is a reassuring thing. It's expensive but most people would not want to be without it. We want a guarantee that we are covered just in case. Insurance is a safety net to catch us and support us if we fall. When I add up the amount I have paid for medical insurance over the years, it could pay for a very nice house. I know the insurance companies have made money on me, but I'm glad we have it. You have the insurance but you hope you won't need it. In fact, I want more insurance categories. If it were available I would be first on line to buy success insurance. I would also like to acquire confidence and achievement insurance and good job insurance, as well as *nachas* insurance. Don't you think popularity insurance would be nice to have?

You cannot be too careful. If you are vigilant, you may find something that is amiss with everything. Most of the foods we eat, for example, have been found to be hazardous to our health. People once assumed that all fruits and vegetables were safe and natural. Now we are warned that some fruits are not safe enough. Some cells in our corn supply have been altered and no one can guarantee that the changes are safe. There is also the fear associated with the unknown effects of the pesticides used in the growing process. Therefore, we are advised to purchase organic fruits and vegetables. Is it ever possible to be certain?

There will always be uncertainty and doubt. It is a part of Hashem's plan for the world. There will always be a "what if." After all, we are only human. There are hundreds of factors that are beyond our control. We aren't even certain what the weather will be tomorrow. Scientists have written enough books about the weather to fill a room and there have been great technological advances, yet they still can't predict tomorrow's weather with certainty. Three years ago a terrible blizzard was predicted in the New York area. Schools closed. Shoppers rushed to stock up on food. Important meetings and events were cancelled. Then the snow began to fall. Instead of the expected 3 feet the total snowfall was about 2 inches. We don't know the future. Only Hashem knows indisputably what is best for us.

Has it ever happened to you? You expected things to happen a certain way and were just about to accomplish your goal, but things didn't happen the way you expected them to. You almost felt that a Divine hand was holding you back. Afterwards you found out that Hashem's ways are wonderful. Your plans failed for your benefit.

These occurrences should fill us with confidence and hope. We may feel that our powers are limited, but that's not a problem because there is an unlimited Power supporting and guiding us. Every day Hashem is taking care of us. We may feel confused, but that's fine because there is a more profound Wisdom watching over us. We may not know what will be, but Hashem knows. Hashem is our source of confidence and hope. Therefore, the best insurance is trust and faith (*bitachon*).

We may pray with fervor for something specific. Yet we may feel a doubt — "Do I know for certain that it is the right thing for me?" So add a prayer for that doubt — Hashem, do what is best and in the best way. You know the future, so please, Hashem, make it a good one.

Flexibility reduces disappointment and frustration.

☙ *Roller Coaster*

*W*e were at the amusement park. We went on one roller-coaster ride after another. We checked our watches and realized that we only had a short time left in the park — departure time was in 20 minutes. Just one more roller coaster ride, we hoped. Impatiently, we waited on the long line for our turn. The line was getting smaller and we could see the roller coaster before us. However, the line was still moving too slowly. It was time to leave. We were disappointed when we turned away.

We watched enviously as the roller coaster climbed slowly to the top. Suddenly, the roller coaster stalled. It couldn't restart. The cars were full of people. They were on the top point right before a huge drop. Those people had to climb out of the car and fearfully climb down. As I watched them, I was grateful that I had been behind them on line. If I had gotten on that roller coaster, I'd be the one that was stuck up there now.

Often in the course of a day we ask, "Why did it happen this way? Why didn't things go the way I wanted? I davened fervently. I tried so hard. Why?" We have to stop and realize that everything that happens is for the best. Hashem's ways are wonderful.

Estie M.

∽๑๐

*T*he chef in our summer camp related the following tale. Each time he tells this story he remembers again the great kindness that Hashem did for him. Nissim was drafted into the Israeli army when he was 18 years old. Since he was an observant Jew it was extremely difficult for him to obtain enough food to eat. He was constantly hungry because he couldn't partake of the non-kosher goodies which the other soldiers enjoyed. One kitchen aide, Michael, felt bad for him and tried to help him whenever possible.

One day he came to Nissim with a special treat. The army had just purchased new utensils and Michael had baked a cake for Nissim in one of the new pans. The cake was therefore kosher because it had only kosher ingredients and nothing had been previously made with these utensils. Nissim was delighted and thanked Michael profusely. He then carefully wrapped the cake and put it away for Shabbos.

That Friday Nissim was standing by the roadside. Suddenly something startled Nissim and he dropped his precious cake. It was instantly covered with dirt. Nissim felt devastated. Was this his reward for struggling to keep kashrus? There was nothing to be done so he sadly continued on his way.

A pale and worried Michael greeted Nissim when he arrived back in camp. He begged Nissim to please forgive him . Nissim was puzzled. Why was Michael apologizing? Michael hesitantly explained that shortly after Nissim had left he realized that he had mistakenly used non-kosher utensils and therefore the cake was not kosher. He felt terrible that he had caused Nissim to sin. Nissim was astounded. A miracle had just occurred that prevented him from *eating something not kosher! With a chuckle he described his experience with the dusty cake to Michael.*

Hashem watches over every Jew.

Malky G.

⚬⚬⚬

Bitachon — Being deeply aware of principles that are the foundations of our life.

Bitachon isn't expensive and doesn't require that we move to a new place. We simply have to change our thoughts. Yet it is often not easy to change the way we evaluate what is happening to us. It can be even more frustrating if we think *bitachon* will be easy. We have to recognize that there is a force almost as strong as gravity pulling us to process what happens according to logic. At times, our world feels like a roller coaster. Our days seem to spin out of control. We have to give ourselves time to make the transition. Looking for Hashem's guidance in our life and in the lives of others takes effort. It's worth it! It is the best experience one can have. It will not only help us feel better but will actually make our life better. We must remember that SOMEONE is driving and steering us in the right direction, always.

✒ *Lost and Found*

When I entered the bookstore I was amazed. There was an entire bookcase of books that focused solely on the holiday of Chanukah. I felt challenged by such a vast collection. The rush to cook and shop for Chanukah had caused me to lose sight of the real Chanukah message. Shouldn't I gain more from the eight days of Chanukah than *latkes* and applesauce? I decided that I would search for eight Torah thoughts for Chanukah. At my weekly lecture, I discussed several insights I had found that penetrated beneath the surface facts of Chanukah. I presented eight thoughts for the eight nights. I focused on gratitude, preparing goals, the power of small actions, and miracles that occur in our lives. The class was winding down.

Mrs. R. shared her experience:

"My husband works with diamond jewelry. He was given a pair of very exclusive diamond earrings on consignment and had promised the supplier that he would pay for them as soon as the pair was sold. One of the earrings was lost and was missing for three months. Everyone in the office hunted for the earring several times. We were in a quandary. How could we afford to pay for the pair if it remained lost? The supplier asked my husband to either return the earrings or sell them. I said, "Don't worry. You'll see that you will find it." My husband requested a few more days from the supplier. We continued looking, although we were feeling discouraged.

"I'll never forget the night it happened. We were getting ready to go to a wedding. My husband saw something sparkling on the floor near the leg of the dresser. He always bends down when he sees something that sparkles even if it's on the sidewalk. It could be glass, but it could also be a diamond. My husband picked the thing up. It was the earring! No one can explain how it got to our house! We had found it!"

As we spoke about earrings Esther touched her ear. "My earring is missing! This is the third pair I've lost this year." Together, we all said the prayer for finding a lost object. Some of us looked near the door and under the table. We didn't find it. We settled down with a sigh to say some Tehillim. Esther left early to reach her afternoon job on time. The bell rang. Esther had returned. She was beaming as she held up something golden and glittering in her hand. "I found my earring in the car. Thank you, everyone."

There was a triumphant climate in the room. Experiencing Esther's fortunate find together made all the concepts in the lecture tangible. We all felt happy for Esther. Just two days before Chanukah we had found Divine Providence glittering right in front of us.

●❖ That Was Close!

As usual, Devorah Klein (name has been changed) spent her summer in Camp Bais Yaakov. The summer progressed smoothly as each new day brought its own excitement and adventure. On the last day, Devorah stood surrounded by her friends discussing post-camp plans. However, Devorah was completely unaware of the danger that lay ahead on that final day of camp.

QUESTION: You witnessed quite a traumatic incident. Can you tell me what happened?

DEVORAH: Well, it was the last day of camp. Campers were scurrying about trying to make sure that their luggage reached the trucks to be loaded. They also worried about getting a good seat on the bus. I was standing outside my bunkhouse, conversing with my friends. The truck stopped just a short distance away and the driver (leaving the truck in park) jumped out to load the truck. Suddenly, the truck started rolling backwards toward my bunkhouse! There were children playing in the truck's path who scrambled quickly to safety. The truck crashed into my bunkhouse, in the exact spot where a girl had stood praying just moments before. Then, as if with a mind of its own, the truck stopped in its tracks. This was surely a miracle since the truck had knocked into a bed in which one of my friends was sleeping. She woke up without even one scratch.

QUESTION: What was your reaction to this shocking scene?

DEVORAH: At first I panicked. I knew that some of my friends were in the bunkhouse at that moment. I was especially nervous for my friend who was sleeping before the truck crashed through.

QUESTION: What did your sleeping friend do when she woke up?

DEVORAH: My friend woke up a bit traumatized. She didn't understand what had happened. She quickly got dressed and came out to everyone. When she walked out of the bunkhouse we all surrounded her. We began dancing and singing, *Chasdei Hashem ki lo samnu* (The kindness of Hashem is without end). It was a beautiful sight that I'll never forget.

QUESTION: What were you thinking when you saw your friend walk out of the bunkhouse without a scratch?

DEVORAH: I couldn't believe it! I would not have imagined that anyone could come out from such an accident without major injuries, or broken limbs, or bruises. Yet my friend emerged without a scratch. It was a total miracle that the truck stopped itself without hitting her or any other girls in the bunkhouse and causing injury, *baruch Hashem.*

QUESTION: What did the bunkhouse look like?

DEVORAH: The truck totally ripped though a section of the wall. The roof above the section was caving in. The rear end of the truck was protruding into the bunkhouse. The wall was wrecked, and the surrounding windows were shattered. All the beds and cubbies in the area were thrown out of place. Everything was smashed. That entire section of the bunkhouse wasn't recognizable.

QUESTION: How did the camp react to the incident?

DEVORAH: The camp reacted in a responsible fashion. The staff cleared the area to make certain that anyone who might need assistance received it. In addition to Hatzolah, the camp nurse came down to check that all the campers involved were okay. Only after the staff had ascertained that there was no immediate danger of the building collapsing did they allow girls to retrieve their possessions from the bunkhouse. Then they sealed off the area altogether. They also spoke to frightened campers and calmed everyone down.

QUESTION: What else did the camp do?

DEVORAH: First of all, they sent out letters to the parents informing them of the accident and their plans to make a *seudas hodaah* this upcoming summer. They also renovated and repaired the bunkhouse.

QUESTION: What did you learn from the experience?

DEVORAH: No matter how much we think we are in control we really have no power. Every detail of our lives is directed from Above. Hashem cares for us with special love. All we have to do is open our eyes and we will clearly see this. The lesson is self-evident. Our every move is directed from Above.

◆ *In Dangerous Territory*

Every morning the first words I say are the *Modeh Ani* prayer: "Thank You, Hashem, living and eternal King, for You have returned my soul within me with compassion, great is Your faithfulness." When I was 4, I listened wide-eyed as my teacher explained that every morning when we open our eyes we experience a miracle. When you go to sleep at night your soul leaves your body. When you wake up it's not because of the alarm clock. Hashem has personally returned your soul and granted you the gift of life. I wonder if this concept has remained real for me or if I just recite the prayer by rote.

Something that most of us don't really think about became a reality for this particular family. It began as an innocent drive through the countryside in a rented car. They never anticipated the danger that could surround them in an instant.

QUESTION: Where were you when your harrowing experience took place?

ANSWER: We were traveling in Israel. Our family was spending the entire Succos holiday together in Jerusalem. On Chol HaMoed, my husband and I planned to do some touring with the family. We intended to show our children some of the holy and beautiful sites of Israel. It was early afternoon when we were actually attacked.

QUESTION: Please describe what happened.

ANSWER: My husband made some wrong turns, since he was not familiar with the Israeli highways. Before we knew it, we were in a strange territory. We had no clue which direction to take to get back to a familiar road. A group of Palestinian teenagers suddenly approached our car from the back and began throwing huge boulders. I screamed to the kids, "On the floor! Get down on the floor." We crouched, huddled together on the floor of the van. Rocks crashed through the windows. Shards of glass were everywhere. My husband pressed down hard on the accelerator and we just drove without knowing where we were going. Eventually, we found our way back to a Jewish town, *baruch Hashem*.

QUESTION: Was anyone injured?

ANSWER: Everyone got cuts and bruises. Some of my children needed stitches, but *baruch Hashem* no one was hurt seriously. We have a lot to be grateful for.

QUESTION: What were some of the miracles involved?

ANSWER: First and most important no one was hurt too badly, *baruch Hashem*. Another miracle was that my baby was not strapped into his car seat, because then I wouldn't have been able to unstrap him quickly enough, G-d forbid. He was especially vulnerable to the huge rocks coming in through the windows. It was also a miracle that the driver's window was the only window that wasn't shattered. If that window had been hit, how would we have escaped? I don't like to think about that.

QUESTION: How did your life change?

ANSWER: We definitely don't take anything for granted anymore. When people in the family return home safely from any trip, we are grateful. It's always a miracle. We have enemies everywhere and every time we are not harmed it's a miracle. We must all be aware of that.

QUESTION: How did you define the word miracle before this experience?

ANSWER: Before I actually lived through a miracle I didn't think about them very much. I just accepted daily occurrences as part of life. I didn't spend too much time thinking about it.

QUESTION: Did your perspective on miracles change?

ANSWER: I now view everything, every ordinary day, as a miracle. I feel that safety and security are a gift coming to us directly from Hashem, wrapped in His love. Hashem is always there protecting us and shielding us with His miracles, which are constant.

QUESTION: What lesson can we all learn from your experience?

ANSWER: Look for Hashem's miracles in good times. If you train yourself to search for the positive, you'll begin noticing it. This will help you look at your life with a different perspective. Your days will become more pleasant.

❧

The only possible response when one realizes that Hashem has given him a second chance is overwhelming gratitude. You feel it in a way that is different than anything you can hear, read, or learn about. The perception of Hashem's direct love can't be captured in words. It's an intensely joyous feeling that surrounds your heart.

Some people are never the same after they experience a miracle. Other people slide back into routine. The challenge is to remember Hashem's kindness.

The Missing Piece

Our mind swirls with questions. They drag us down. We try to push them away but sometimes they keep us up at night. We search for things to do that will help us forget our questions. Questions make us feel tired even when we've just woken up. We search for answers only to find that those who we thought knew everything feel confused too. There are the big questions that we are almost afraid to mention. Questions of life and death, peace, health and families remaining intact haunt us. Yet smaller questions bother us, too.

Why? Why did my friend act that way? Why did the teacher make the girl cry? My relatives promised to come and then they left me waiting. I tried so hard, but the camp said no. I waited for the "magic" envelope from the seminary but it didn't come. Why does my neighbor still owe me the babysitting money? These questions can drain our energy. Shaindy has a way to bypass these questions. The ideas presented by Shaindy may be something you knew before. However, the familiar experience that taught her these ideas is sure to make you smile.

⟡

It was my tenth birthday and I received a 1,000-piece puzzle as a gift. For weeks I worked on the puzzle. Every day I spent some time with it. First I found all the outside pieces and made the frame. Afterwards I sorted the pieces by color. I patiently worked on each section. I was looking forward to finally being able to hang up my masterpiece.

I was almost finished. The last few dozen pieces were easier to place. Things were starting to fill in. Just a few more pieces and the picture would be complete. At last there was only one empty space left, and then the puzzle would be complete. To my dismay the piece was gone! I searched in every corner of the room to no avail. I felt frustrated — after weeks of work my picture was not complete.

Eventually I got over my initial disappointment and life resumed its regular routine. The puzzle was almost completely forgotten. It lay under my bed gathering dust. Pesach was drawing near and the cleaning began. One day, while I was cleaning behind the china closet I found it. A tiny, dusty, smudged puzzle piece lay in a pile of dirt.

I took the piece and gently dusted it off. This essential piece would complete the picture. I ran to my room and placed this missing piece in the waiting space. I finally could hang the completed puzzle on the wall over my bed. However, first I traced that missing little piece onto a paper and hung it near my bed, too.

Now when I walk into my room after a day full of doubt, questions and disappointments I see a gentle reminder to keep things in perspective. I see the little puzzle piece.

The "missing" piece reminds me that this world has missing pieces. We can't see the complete beautiful picture because we are missing a piece. Hashem has that missing piece and He will complete the picture at some future date. Until then our picture can't be complete. That piece is my reminder. It calms me and helps to remind me of where I am time and time again.

Shaindy K.

⋙⋘

Life is often confusing. There are so many things that we can't understand — something is missing. Sometimes months or years later we do find the missing piece. We finally realize one tiny detail and we are able to reach a new understanding. All of our questions do have an answer. Some answers are revealed to us, while others remain hidden. In the meantime we can only wait and look to Hashem with patience and trust.

Chapter 11

The Gift of
Beginning Anew

New Beginnings

Always bear in mind that your own resolution to succeed is more important than any other thing.

(Abraham Lincoln)

It is said that every beginning is hard. Before starting something for the first time one must plan ahead. You might consider what you are getting yourself into, how to approach it, and what the best way is to reach your goal.

Before the new school year began I lost a lot of sleep. I had butterflies in my stomach because of my nervous anticipation. Even though I had a few close friends I felt nervous. I worried about changes that might have occurred over the summer.

Would my friends still like me? Will all my friends still be in my class? What if the school decided to mix up all the classes? Who will be in my class? Would I like my teachers? Even more important — would they like me? For many nights I would lie awake worrying. Different scenarios would dance in my head. By the time the first day of school arrived I felt sick.

I worked to combat this fear and I finally realized that many of my worries were actually for no reason. I realized that if I approached the situation in a different way I would be more calm. I began with a simple attitude adjustment. Instead of looking at this period as a new year, I would look at it as a continuation from the past year. Even if some friends are in a different class, I'll surely have a few friends with me. I thought about the past years. In the past most of the teachers liked me. I realized I was silly to worry. After all, I'm a likable person. As I began turning my worries around, the beginning of the year became less frightening.

It is true that new beginnings are difficult but with a proper perspective they can also be enjoyable. Beginning anew can be something to look forward to. Just put a smile on your face and you are halfway there already.

Malky O.

∽๑෴

Moving — Starting Over

The announcement came when you weren't expecting it. You were sitting at the supper table looking down at the peas in your plate. Suddenly your father said, "I have something important to tell you." You looked up and both of your parents were smiling nervously. You wondered, "Is my grandmother coming to visit? Is the family going to Israel for Pesach? What will the news be?" You were looking intently at both parents, trying to find a clue. Then your father said three words that changed your life—"We are moving!"

Maybe you didn't hear correctly. This cannot be true. Your world seems to be crumbling in front of you. What will you do? Why didn't anyone ask you? Children should also have a say. You feel shocked. How will you survive?

Moving is frightening. You feel like the rug has been pulled out from under your feet. There were so many plans in your heart. There were so many things you looked forward to. It's horrifying to think that now those plans are gone. What about your friends? It will be difficult to say good-bye. Although you always complained about going to school you miss school already when you imagine having to start all over in a new one.

There are so many terrifying questions that seem to have no answer. Will the teachers be strict? Will the girls be mean? What will the new place be like? Will you ever see your old friends again?

Change is not easy. You don't want to face the challenge of the unknown. Deep down, however, you know you can handle it. True, it's difficult to leave old friends, but you will find new ones. You coped in the past and with Hashem's help you will deal with this. After all, it's only a move to a new city. There are still phones and fax machines. You won't be that far away. An occasional visit is still possible. You don't have to learn a new language or adjust to a new culture. There is also the secure thought that your parents are taking care of every last detail of your life. There will be a new house for the family and a new job for your father. There will be shuls and schools and a community.

$$\sim\!\circ\!\sim$$

What follows is a story about Mrs. Green. Mrs. Green was born in Krula, Hungary. World War II destroyed every remnant of the place where she was born. The homes, the shuls, the schools, and most importantly, the people were all gone. After a brief stay in Hungary she moved to Austria. Her family lived in Austria for two years and then they moved to Brazil. After fourteen years in Brazil they moved to New York.

Moving is difficult. This woman adjusted to new countries, new cultures and new languages several times. Yet in each new place, she not only settled in and succeeded, she also looked for ways to open her home and heart to others. Cooking, raising money, preparing cake and challah for dozens of poor families, and inviting guests were just a few of the ways Mrs. Green helped others.

Perhaps the most difficult change one might ever have to adjust to is suddenly entering a hospital. When illness strikes, one may find oneself in the most uninviting surroundings possible. The doctors and nurses use terminology that is difficult to understand. There is endless poking and prodding. The food is not palatable. The bed has a plastic mattress. One cannot sleep because lights are on, phones are ringing and the halls are filled with activity and pacing people. Perhaps because Mrs. Green understood the trauma of moving she devoted many years to helping patients in hospitals.

ESTY: What was Bubby's life like before the war?

MOMMY: Bubby was born in Krula, Hungary. When she was little her mother sent her to visit old people who didn't have anyone to help them. She lit the fire, cleaned up and helped in any way they needed. She was only 9 or 10 at the time, a young girl.

ESTY: What did she do right after the war? Did she return to her hometown?

MOMMY: She married your grandfather who came from the same hometown as she did. She remained there for a few years. As a young couple, their house was full of guests. They helped out orphans and poor people. There used to be a ball game in town. Bubby stood in the scorching heat selling cold drinks to raise money for the needy. After her first two children were born she moved to Austria. From there she traveled to Bolivia where I was born. Then we settled in Brazil. We lived there for fourteen years.

ESTY: What was life like in Brazil?

MOMMY: We were the first ones to wear long sleeves and to dress modestly. Kosher food was hard to acquire. Every Friday

When one takes this journey one experiences more than a change of scenery. Everything is different in Meah Shearim. In Brooklyn one walks on pavement, while in Meah Shearim one treads on cobblestones. The houses are not of red brick, instead they are of white stone. One does not see cars zoom by on wide parkways marked with double yellow lines. Instead the buses inch through narrow alleyways. While the streets in Brooklyn have numbers and letters, the winding roads and courtyards of Meah Shearim have names.

The journey to Meah Shearim is more than a trip to a different place. When one steps through the narrow arch and enters a courtyard in Meah Shearim one enters a different era. The 20th century seems far, far away.

～∂ᴄ～

*I*n the holy city, the air and the surroundings were conducive to *a life of tranquility. When one walked the streets one was aware that years ago our ancestors had traveled on these same streets. Many gathered here to bring sacrifices to Hashem. Now people walked upon these same cobblestone streets with a sense of history and even humility. All week long people rushed, busy with their everyday lives, although there was a special feeling in the air. However, when Shabbos came the holiness flooded in. Not only did you feel the holiness but your faith in Hashem was tangible.*

It was wartime, a difficult period for "Babba" — my grandmother Devorah — since her husband was in America at the time. Babba took her children over to her sister-in-law Chana who lived in a safer location with her parents. In that one small apartment were three families: Chana, her parents, Babba, and their children.

One morning Chana sent her daughter Fraydel to buy some milk. One of Babba's children, 7-year-old Faigele, decided to go along. Faigele opened the door, slipped out, and ran after her cousin Fraydel. However, by the time Faigele got outside Fraydel was out of sight. She began running across the field.

Suddenly the air-raid siren sounded, warning all to take shelter. Not knowing what to do, Faigele fell to the ground, hoping the tall grass would hide her. She remained in this hidden position for a short interval. Then she got up and ran home. When Faigele returned home she witnessed something that she never forgot.

Everyone had run into the "shelter," a stone room in the basement without any windows, everyone except for Zeida, Reb Yaakov Meir Shechter. He was sitting and eating peacefully while his wife pleaded with him to come to safety. Zeida had a firm and unbroken practice never to get up from a meal from the moment he washed until after completing the entire bentching, and now was no exception. When Zeida finished eating he recited bentching as usual, pronouncing every syllable carefully and precisely. Once he was done, Zeida got up and went into the shelter. Seconds later a bomb went off nearby, shattering the window in the next room. A piece of shrapnel hit the exact spot where Zeida had been sitting. The fiery shrapnel continued on and landed on one of the sefarim from which Zeida had been learning. This Torah book has remained with us as a reminder for the family. Zeida would refer to the sefer and tell the family, "Nothing happens without it being decreed from Hashem. Every decree has its time and place." Babba was raised with faith and passed it on to her children.

One day when Babba was in her mid-20s she went shopping for some household items. She had only a little money, which she had saved up from working. While passing a grocery which her grandmother used to shop in, Babba decided to enter. She asked the owner if her grandmother owed money. Babba knew that her grandmother hated to owe people anything and now that she wasn't alive she could not repay her debts. The owner told her that there was a small bill outstanding. It was almost the exact amount of money Babba had in her pocket. After an inner battle, Babba made a decision. She put aside her needs and paid her grandmother's bill. That night the grandmother came to her in a dream. Her face was glowing and she was hold-

ing two things. In one hand was a big silver plate with a challah on it and in the other a bag of baby clothing. She told Babba, "Here, take these, you will need them." Nine months later (after several years of not having any children) my grandparents became proud parents. A cousin who was also childless had a boy around the same time — the tray with challah!

Babba was a young woman in her 30s when she first came to America in 1951. She had a devoted husband. To support the family my grandfather had traveled to America and was away many weeks at a time. It had been difficult for Babba to run from home to home and shelter to shelter on her own with three children. After much debating and asking a rav she decided to move to America.

Life was different in America. One day of the week was especially difficult — Shabbos. In Israel when Shabbos arrived everything stopped. On Shabbos morning, men, women and children all strolled home from shul through the streets. All you saw was the men in their shtreimlach and women with white silk kerchiefs covering their heads. The boys wore velvet hats with neatly curled payos. The girls wore simple dresses and had their hair braided in two braids with ribbon tied on the end of each braid. In America the streets were full of traffic, and most stores were open. She felt pain in her heart about this situation, but there was nothing else she could have done.

Although life was different in America, Babba held on to her values. Even in America she lived the same way as she had in Israel. She always thought about others before herself. She adhered to her principles. She had four children and many grandchildren and great-grandchildren.

Chava Esty E.

❧❧

Grandmothers' stories are more than shared memories. These descriptions of the holy city where Babba grew up and the unique rituals of her family have created a legacy. The sights that Babba never forgot weave a tapestry of tradition. Although her children live in Brooklyn they walk in the paths of their ancestors. They carry a part of the atmosphere of Meah Shearim into the future. And so it is for each one of us who retain our families' traditions.

From Dreams to Reality

If we all did the things we are capable of doing we would literally astonish ourselves.

(Thomas Alva Edison)

If your self-discipline matched your dreams what wonderful things would you do? Perhaps you would begin a diet tomorrow. It's possible that you would sign up for art class — tomorrow. You would definitely say the bedtime *Shema* with greater concentration — tomorrow. The assigned report would be perfect, but you would begin it tomorrow. Someone asked you to visit an elderly woman on your block and you intend to visit — tomorrow.

In a secret recess of our heart there are many plans. We have all had grand dreams. However, it's a struggle to begin. We tend to postpone action. We tell ourselves that we will do something as soon as we can. Unfortunately, we become busy and forget our great intentions.

Why do we wait to act on our plans? Sometimes we have inner doubts. For years we have believed that change is hard work. Before we even begin something, we feel that it will be difficult. We fear the pain of failure or rejection. However, if we don't put the things we really want to do first on our list there will always be something else to do. Those little things tend to gobble up our time and our dreams.

What are some of the thought patterns of procrastinators?

Admiration from a distance: You see that a friend has "adopted" a lonely girl in the class. You really admire her. She has such a kind heart. You think, "I should do that too, one of these days. I wish I could be as patient. Oh, well. It's just not for me." You sigh and walk away.

Envy: You've always wanted to learn how to draw. Your classmate's sketches look good enough for a picture frame. You think, "If only I could draw like that. I should have gone to the art course. I'll never draw as well as her in any case." Envy ruins your potential pleasure in life. It's like a black cloud that blocks your view of what you can accomplish.

Expecting perfection instantly: You hear an inspiring lecture and resolve, "No *lashon hara* from now on." Two days later you slip and talk about someone because they got you really angry. You experience inner conflict between what you want to do and what you actually do. "I'll never overcome the temptation to speak *lashon hara,* so I might as well give up," you conclude.

Total perfection isn't a realistic goal. When you think you must be perfect then a mistake makes you feel like a failure. Instead, look for ways that you have improved and focus on that. Even if the improvement is limited, you can feel that you have accomplished something valuable.

Tomorrow: You write letters but they remain in your drawer. You pass the lonely lady on your block and promise that you'll visit — sometime. You know your classmate has mono and you put off visiting for so long that she comes back to school. One of these days you will do it. Sometimes you even begin, but then many tomorrows pass before you decide to finish. Saying that you'll do it tomorrow is like driving a car with the brakes on. Don't postpone things — act NOW!

Empty promises: It's hard to say no, so you promise to help. In your heart you know you won't be able to keep that promise, but you don't have the strength to argue now. When the time comes you find you are too busy so you give the person an excuse. Try to avoid making commitments you cannot keep. In the long run it will be better for everyone. Don't be afraid or embarrassed to say "No" when necessary.

➥ *Tomorrow*

Tomorrow.
Those three syllables can mean so much.
Tomorrow.
That is the time to achieve my goals.

That is the time to do many mitzvos.
Tomorrow.
I'll write a letter to my lonely aunt.
I'll visit the nursing home.
Tomorrow.
I'll help my friend study for a math regent.
I won't let a word of *lashon hara* pass my lips or enter my mind.
I'll *daven* with special intensity.
Tomorrow.

Tomorrow arrives. As usual, I rush out of bed, throw on my clothes, mumble what's supposed to be a *brachah*, gulp down a couple of spoons of cereal, scoot out the door and run to school.

For the first half of the day, I am busy with so much work. We have a guest speaker. The speaker takes longer than usual. Recess disappears. During lunch, I try to cram in seventeen pages of notes for that *Navi* final. A voice whispers something about *chesed*. Who has time? I didn't even eat my lunch!

In the afternoon, I finally satisfy my grumbling stomach and eat. After school, I rush home, do my homework, help my mother with my younger sibling, take a shower and drift off to sleep.

Day in, day out, I always seem too busy to do all that I had planned. Every day I find myself saying,

"I'll surely do it—tomorrow."
Tomorrow. Will it ever arrive?
Will I ever find the time?

Gitty Skolnik

Helpful ideas to overcome procrastination:

Learn from the person you admire — Perhaps the person you admire has discovered ideas along the way that would help you achieve your goals. Instead of anxiously striving and being frustrated, find out "the secret." Perhaps when you discover the pleasure that this person whom you admire gains from the good things she does you'll want to do them too.

I learned: _____

From:_____

Turn Your Envy Into Action — There will never be another you. It's important to remember that. On occasion you may imagine that others are better equipped than you are. Don't try to be someone else. Just be the best you can be. If you want to learn a new skill think of a way you can pursue it that will be a pleasure, not a pain. Proceed slowly and enjoy your progress.

List three things you like to do that you can improve :

1. _____
2. _____
3. _____

It's not too late if you start now — How many dreams of yesterday have dissipated before they became reality? Instead of waiting for tomorrow, begin now. We carefully craft our plans but in the meantime nothing happens. Do something small today or this week. Send out that thank-you card. Find out the details that will help you begin the project. A small success leads to a larger one.

Today I will: _____

_____

Keep your promise — We believe that making a promise is good by itself. Actually, a promise is only good if we keep it. If all we had to do to develop our capabilities was make a promise, everything would be different. Everyone on earth would be successful and happy. In reality, there is usually a gap between our dreams and our deeds. The way to close that gap is by setting goals that you can keep. You can't succeed if you don't get out there and act. The *yetzer hara* keeps us busy thinking instead of doing.

Even if you want to break a habit — even if you want to reach a goal — even if it's been hard in the past trying to motivate yourself, you can do the things you want to do without pain and strain. Hashem has promised us that if we make a small effort He will bless us with success in great measure. However, your small effort must be sincere and you have to persist. Many experienced cooks can look back at the first challah they baked. When they began it tasted really heavy, but they persisted, the family was patient and quite soon the recipe was perfect. You can do this, too! Don't give up!

Mitzvos in a Minute

Here are twenty-one mitzvos you can do anywhere in a minute. Some of these ideas are based on tape 720 by R' Avigdor Miller.

1. Spend at least 30 seconds thinking about the World to Come. We are in this world only as a preparation for the next world. This is the purpose of life.
   (Shabbos is 1/60th of the World to Come, so you can spend some seconds thinking about your favorite Shabbos moments. As you ponder that joy reflect on the fact that the joy of *Olam Haba* will be infinitely greater.)

2. Spend a few seconds each day saying, "Hashem, I love You!" You will be fulfilling a positive commandment from the Torah. Hashem is listening. He loves you much more than you love Him.

3. Do one random act of kindness. Kindness is one of the three foundations of the world. Examples: put something away in its proper place, push something to the side of the sidewalk so no one will slip on the "banana peel," let someone make that left turn, smile. Even easy acts of kindness count.

4. Encourage someone every day. Hashem encourages the humble. Send anonymous letters of kindness, give a clerk a compliment, call someone who is home alone.

5. Spend one minute today thinking about what happened yesterday. This is a simple way to accomplish the mitzvah of *teshuvah*.

6. Once a day say, "I am doing this in order to be more aware of G-d."

7. Be aware of the principle: "Man was created in the image of G-d." Every human face is a reflection of G-d. Your face is like a screen and your soul is like a projector which projects

on your face the soul within. Your soul contains a spark of G-d's greatness.

8. Once a day give a person a full smile. We pray that just as we smile at others, G-d should smile down upon us.

9. Thank G-d for your clothes.

10. Thank G-d for the gift of sight.

11. Thank G-d that you can move about freely.

12. Thank G-d that you can stand erect.

13. Pray for Jerusalem. Think about Jerusalem in its glory when the Temple stood.

14. Visualize an apple, orange, pear or other fruit and think about the Creator's wisdom in creating it.

15. Thank G-d for today — not just in the morning, but throughout the day.

16. Say the *Shema* — Hear O Israel, Hashem is our G-d, Hashem the One and Only.

17. Think of a time when G-d saved your life.

18. Think of any of the Ten Plagues. It is a positive commandment to remember that G-d took us out of Egypt.

19. When you take a drink of water and say the blessing "all exists by G-d's word," pause for a moment and include everything in that expression. You can focus on a worry that is weighing upon you or on a simple thing that has gone well for you. It's all from G-d's word.

20. When you say Amen to a blessing it includes:
    A — God is (K)ei-l, the Creator
    M — Melech, G-d is King and He watches over the world now.
    N — Neeman, G-d will faithfully keep all His promises for the future.

21. Instead of saying, "Today is Monday," "Today is Tuesday," once a day say, "Today is the second day from Shabbos," "Today is the third day from Shabbos." Every time you count the days from Shabbos it is a mitzvah.

The Gift
of Family
and Tradition

Coming Home

An anecdote is told about a post-war refugee family transferred from place to place in search of settlement. On one occasion, the family was standing in a train station surrounded by their tattered suitcases, boxes and bags when a bystander approached the family's 6-year-old daughter and remarked, "You poor darling, moving about so much with no place to call home."

The little girl looked up in surprise. "You are mistaken," she replied. "I do have a home. I just don't have a house to put it into."

(Reb. Fayge Twerski)

Every girl wishes she had a perfect relationship with her mother. You think back to the day when you received your first *siddur* in Pre-1A. Mother was so proud of you as she took a picture with glistening eyes. She was always praising your tiny accomplishments and forgiving your small lapses. What happened in the past ten years?

It seems now that your mother and you have nothing in common. You seem to have opposite tastes in clothes. Your mother doesn't understand why you go to sleep late or skip breakfasts. You have a different outlook on important issues. She doesn't always agree with your choice of friends, how you spend your spare time, or even how you style your hair. There seems to be a canyon separating the two of you. How can you create a bridge?

Mothers and daughters can be poles apart. You have different priorities. You like to do different things. You come home from school really enthusiastic about something and eager to share it with your mother. She nods her head but you can tell by the way she is looking at you that she doesn't see it in the same way you do. You begin to think that your mother and you are like night and day.

Differences don't have to lead to a rift between you. There are two simple words that can bridge the gap. Those two words are "Thank you." Every day expend some effort into showing your appreciation. Keep an open mind. Notice the major things that are alike about the two of you despite your differences. You may want to be yourself and assert your identity, but you can still smile and express your gratitude.

❧

❧ Thank You, Mother

I look back and see how far I've come. Mother, you saw my first smile. Why did I smile? It was because you were smiling at me. You saw my first steps. I stumbled into your outstretched arms.

I grew older. Now I was no longer a toddler but a young child. Running with a paper clutched in my hand, I rushed to show you my artwork. I loved the way your face would light up with pride and love as you examined the colorfully scribbled paper.

I matured and became a young teenager. Whether it was problems with friendships, teachers, or life in general, it was to you, Mother, that I ran. You listened and gave me encouragement, advice and support.

Now my days are filled with school and friends. I realize these years will not last forever. One day I will be busy with a home of my own and children to take care of. I want to look back at these years and be happy with the way I used them. I don't want to be disappointed at opportunities I missed.

Mother, I want to express my gratitude. You are and always will be a part of my life. You help me and guide me. I hope I will be half as good a mother as you are to me. Thank you for everything.

Estee G.

∽ↄↄ∾

When I was about 15, I learned about the importance of nutrition. I remember walking into the kitchen eager to share my newfound knowledge. "Mommy, you shouldn't drink so much coffee. We learned that the caffeine is really bad for you."

My mother looked at me thoughtfully. "Well, there was one period in my life when I drank absolutely no coffee. Not even a tablespoon."

"When was that?" I asked wonderingly, because my mother really drinks a lot of coffee.

"Well, before you were born, the doctor told me to watch very carefully what I ate. He warned me that coffee would have to be eliminated from my diet. So I stopped drinking coffee for half a year. It's amazing what we'll do for a baby that we wouldn't do for ourselves."

Hashem endowed parents with feelings of tenderness and compassion toward their children. A child is a part of his father. The father's hope is centered on this child. Do we not see this? Do we not see that the parent will give his child, preference in regard to food, drink, clothing? Parents rush to protect their children from harm. A parent is hurt more by an insult to this child than by an insult to himself. To provide comfort for the child, the burden of toil and weariness is lightly borne by the parent. The Torah teaches children the duty of devotedly serving and honoring their parents.

(Chovos HaLevavos, "Shaar Avodas Elokim")

❧❧❧

❧ *Words of Gratitude*

Mothers find delight in hearing the two simple words — "Thank you." It doesn't take much for a daughter to do this for her mother. This can make your mother's day. All you have to say is two simple words. I don't think that it's difficult. Decide to compliment your mother on the supper she prepares every night. Show enthusiastic appreciation when she buys you something new, even if it's just a uniform shirt. Tell her you enjoyed listening to the music she had on when you came home. Acknowledge the hours she spends listening to you. Whenever your mother does something for you, do this for her — express your gratitude.

Thank her too for the things she has done for you in the past. Remember the endless nights she stayed up with you when you were younger. Remember that she often prevented you from getting hurt physically or emotionally. Thank her for teaching through example and helping you to understand things better. Thank her for helping you even when you didn't deserve it. Appreciate all the times she cared.

How do you think you've grown to be who you are? Your mother has put her life into you since you were born. Actually, just for the fact that she gave birth to you, you owe her your life. However, I'm not telling you to do something difficult. I'm just telling you to say "Thank you" — that's it.

Malkie S. and Mimi S.

❧❧❧

Alphabet Acrostic

Create an upbeat poem about everyone's favorite person — your mother. You can write it on a simple piece of loose-leaf paper or in a lovely card. Perhaps you can make a magnet out of it. Any way you do it, it will be a welcome gift.

Here is an alphabet acrostic:

Thank you, Mother, for going out of your way for me all the time!

Thank you, Mother, for:

Always being there for me.
Being ready to understand.
Calming me when I'm upset.
Doing thousands of loads of laundry.
Every day you pack my lunch.
Forgetting the things I've done wrong.
Going out of your way for me at any time.
Hauling groceries home from the store.
Inviting me into your bed when I had bad dreams.
Joking when I'm sad to cheer me up.
Keeping all my arts and crafts projects from when I was little.
Listening.
Making me feel good about myself.
Noticing my accomplishments — big and small.
Outstanding meals.
Purchasing so many different things for me.
Quietly and gently rebuking me.
Reading a story to me before bed when I was little.
Sending me to good *frum* schools.
Teaching me what's right.
Unending patience.
Vacuuming my room.
Waking me up every morning.
Xtra attention when I needed it.
Your unconditional love.
Zorging [worrying] about me.

Dassy G.

✑ Thank you, Mother

*M*others are very special people. My mother is especially so. My mother is kind, warm and willing to do whatever she can to make her children happy. But there is one specific thing that makes my mother more special than most mothers.

About a year and a half ago, I went to summer camp. When I came home, I faced a difficult choice. Most girls my age do not have to make this decision. Since I live out of town I decided that I wanted to go away to school for the rest of my high school "career." I was not happy in the school I was presently enrolled in, so I decided to go to New York to try to find a school that would be better for me. As soon as I made this decision I told my mother. She was quite shocked at first and I was afraid she would not give me permission. I am her oldest child and I knew it would be hard for her to send me away. But when I told her why I wanted to go, without blinking an eye, she said I could go since I felt it was the right choice.

Looking back, I can imagine that this was a very hard thing for my mother to do. Most mothers would never consider sending their children away until it came time to send them to seminary or yeshivah, or until it was time to marry them off. I thank my mother for being so encouraging about this decision, which would forever change my life in many ways.

Yiskah E.

✑ Thank You, Mother

*S*ometimes in life when you want to say thank you, it is very hard to find the right words to express your gratitude. A mother has a difficult job, but to be the mother of a baalas teshuvah is an even greater challenge. Therefore, Mom, I just hope these words will serve as a token of my gratitude. Thank you

Mother for agreeing to things that made very little sense to you in order that I should be happy.

Even as I remember the times you scolded me and told me to busy myself with other, more useful, things, I know you did it because of your love. I understand that if my child came home and told me that he wanted to start practicing Hinduism, I would react in the same way. No matter how strange I appeared in your eyes, you made an effort to understand.

Without understanding the whole beauty of Shabbos you began to keep Shabbos. You did it so nicely. I will never forget how you started cooking three days in advance. That will always serve as a great lesson to me.

I know that if you had been given a yeshivah education you would keep each mitzvah in the same loving way that you keep Shabbos. You do mitzvos on the basis of simple faith, which I feel is essentially a higher level than mine.

Rachel K.

✒ *Under the Pillow*

Dear Mommy,

It's just an ordinary Tuesday and you are probably surprised to find this letter under your pillow. I just wanted to tell you something very important.

Thank you.

Thank you for being my Mommy. Thank you for the pre-school graduations you attended. I remember wondering why you cried. Thank you for all the kisses you gave me when you thought I was asleep. You didn't forget to put extra mayonnaise in my sandwich because that's how I like it. You patiently wake me up again and again so that I won't be late for school and get detention. You pray for me every day. For all of these things I thank you.

It sounds so inadequate. Please realize, Mommy, how much feeling I am putting into these two simple words.
Thank you!

Love
Your daughter, Shaindy S.

P.S. Please wake me up early. Guess what? I got detention again.

৯৵

It often happens that we say thank you, but that does not necessarily help us feel more in touch with those who are close to us. We may acknowledge all the little things that make our life better but we do not truly feel appreciative. A relationship will not improve if our words are detached and lack meaning. When we decide to grow in our gratitude, it involves much more than mere words of thanks.

We should strive to link thought and sincere feeling to our words and deeds. One path to open our hearts is to remember major events. When a major event occurs we may experience strong feelings of appreciation. We can think about those events and recall how we felt then. This can help us duplicate that feeling in the present.

৯৵

☙ *Foundations*

I vaguely remember the names of the speakers, but do I remember a word of the commencement address at my graduation?

Before graduation, I stood clustered together with my school friends. Afterwards the room was filled with circles of students surrounded by family members. Each of us stood surrounded by the warm embrace of family. I don't remember anything except the smiles of pride on my parents' faces and the excited congratulations of sisters, brothers, aunts and uncles, and saying thank you and smiling. At that moment those two words are not enough to express even a hundredth of how one feels. Parents are the real heroes of a graduation. But I realized then that parents are our heroes every day. I resolved then to say thank you on ordinary days as well.

Graduation is a great day. It is not a frequent event. On your graduation day you may look back and think about all the people that brought you to this day of triumph.

We were all in the car driving to Manhattan. I looked out the window and saw the Manhattan skyline. I felt awed by the sight of the many towering skyscrapers. What gives them the ability to stand so tall and majestic? How are they able to penetrate the sky with their massive height? What is the secret of their strength?

The answer lies deep beneath the ground. Sturdy concrete beams that are in the foundation give the looming skyscrapers their sturdy substructure. Furthermore the strength of these edifices is determined by the quality of the building materials that formed and molded them. Without these tremendous hidden pillars, the impressive structure would crumble.

I am your dear daughter and you are a master architect, Mother. You have laid the foundation of my life. With your sincere, devoted, caring personality and motherly love you established the basis of who I am today.

How do I even begin to express my gratitude? Day after day you have nurtured me, raised me and helped me develop and mature. How do I thank you for always being there when I needed you? Who can measure the value of a kind, encouraging or comforting word? Your wise, experienced advice guided me through confusion. You are a shoulder to lean on and a shelter of security when I feel overwhelmed. You give me all that I need.

The list goes on endlessly. For eighteen years you have given of yourself to make me the person that I am today. How do I begin to express my gratitude for all of this? Words — they are mere droplets of ink. They are completely inadequate to capture what I feel. I can only attempt to say: Thank you. I love you.

Blimie G.

Tradition

I am absolutely not old. My grandmother wasn't old until her last day, and she passed away at the age of 89. Yet I have my moments of nostalgia. Don't you have to be old to reminisce? Well, I'll be young and reminisce.

I remember when a notebook was just a notebook. There was just one kind — the marble composition notebooks. They were bound with stitching down the middle. If you tore out a page in the front, a page fell out in the back. I remember the first spiral notebooks. I was in fourth or fifth grade when they appeared on the shelves in the small stationery store. Now one could tear out a page and the notebook stayed in one piece.

Once there were only two or three varieties of shampoo. Snacks were limited. I grew up on plain potato chips and pretzels. Perhaps on special occasions there were chocolates from Switzerland or Israel. I was fascinated when fruit roll-ups first appeared on the shelves. At the time they only came in apricot flavor. Yogurt came in just three flavors, too — plain, strawberry and blueberry. Perhaps it took us less time to shop in those days.

On Thursday I went shopping for Shabbos. My mother gave me a $20 bill and I brought back change.

Where have the small local groceries gone? What happened to the corner deli? You ordered a hot dog and they asked you if you wanted mustard and sauerkraut. Where has the small candy store gone — where I went with my father on *Motza'ei Shabbos* for a malted?

I would walk into a store and they knew my grandmother, cousins and uncle. Now when I walk into a store I have to show my driver's license.

Once there were no fax machines. A tape recorder worked with spools instead of cassettes. The camera lens had to be manually adjusted and sometimes children would walk away from the "perfect picture" by the time you had it in focus. Instead of a calculator there was a huge black adding machine that needed a table top. It clicked and banged as the storeowner added up your purchases.

We live in a rapidly changing world, but beneath it all, it's such a comfort that the core of our life is identical to that of generations ago. Jews have hung a uniform *mezuzah* on their doors for 3,000 years. We light the same candles on Friday night, recite the exact words of *Kiddush* and eat the same challah. The challah is baked using our grandmother's recipe. At the Shabbos table we sing the *zemiros* to the tune our grandfathers sang. We have three large round hand made matzos at the *Seder* and we ask the same Four Questions.

Our children learn to read the *aleph-beis* that Moshe Rabbeinu used to write the Torah. The men and boys wear the same *tzitzis* as Rashi. We read from a Torah scroll that is a twin to the one that is 1,000 years old and stands behind a glass case in the museum.

For 3.000 years we have followed the same recipes. This isn't simply about the food we eat, it's about the life we lead.

⁀ᴐᴑ

Devora describes her memories of her grandmother's challah. She takes out the same ingredients and makes a twin challah in her home. Her challos will be similar, but not quite the same:

I can still smell the wonderful fragrance of freshly baked challah in my grandmother's oven, when I walked in on Friday mornings.

I used to go to my grandmother every Friday to watch and help her bake challah. She would knead the dough gently. She would separate a piece so she could make a blessing. Next came my favorite part. My grandmother always said, "Now I need your help, Devora." She would separate the dough into pieces and braid the challah. My grandmother gave me six clumps of dough, which I rolled into long log-shaped pieces. Grandmother would then help me braid the challos. She showed me how to braid them evenly so they would come out looking nice. Afterward I brushed the challos with an egg glaze. This made them shiny.

When I was finished I put them in the oven. Grandmother and I waited and chatted until they were ready. They were care-

fully wrapped and I took two challah loaves home for my family's Shabbos table.

Now I take out the ingredients in my kitchen. I look at the index card and follow grandmother's recipe. I will make the same challos that grandmother used to make with me when I was young. Yet the challos are not the same. There is always one thing missing — the gentle hands of my grandmother.

Devora B.

❧

☙ Welcome!

What can you do to comfort yourself when the stress in life mounts and seems like a solid impenetrable wall?

The connection between the generations is simple yet profound. Weekly hours spent together give energy and a perspective to grow on. A grandmother welcomes you and lifts your spirits. She's so obviously happy with you just as you are.

Welcome! She opens the door to her home. She also opens the door to her heart. Come! Learn! Grow! Find sustenance.

Grandmothers don't seem to have to work hard to relax. Their life has a mature perspective. We probably never notice their difficulties because they are so good at hiding them. One would never know the pain of arthritis that hides behind a sunny smile. The perspective that a grandchild's visit is a treasure makes these moments precious.

Perhaps our fast-paced existence isn't letting us find the peace of mind we crave. Once in a while it's good to simply sit down and listen.

❧

I didn't have the greatest day at school. How could I cheer myself up? I decided to visit my grandmother.

I walked slowly and heard the leaves crunch under my feet as I went in the direction of my grandmother's house. I felt so calm enjoying my walk that I didn't even realize that I had arrived at her threshold. I rang the bell. As I opened the door a delicious smell greeted me. I entered the kitchen. I saw my grandmother's old wrinkled face as she stood under the fluorescent light. The knife knocked against the cutting board as she sliced and cut vegetables. Her counter was covered with a variety of foods. It looked like a take-out store.

When I finally said hello, she jumped. She was so engrossed in cooking for Shabbos that she didn't realize I had entered. She wiped her hands and we sat down to talk. My grandmother insisted that I sample something. I've been trying to watch what I eat, but how could I say no?

I tasted one dish. It was so good. My grandmother has a special touch. She returned to the stove. It was calming to watch her add spices and stir the soup. I offered to help clean up and assured her that the job would be done in half the time.

When I left my grandmother's house I was thoughtful. My grandmother works hard at her cooking but it comes out good. She sees the fruits of her labor.

Simie G.

⌒ﬡ⌒

I am an expert on all kinds of food and places to buy them. I can recommend the best restaurants if you want to eat out, but homemade food is better than store-bought food. Nevertheless, I have never eaten any food as delicious as my grandmother's cooking.

When my parents are on vacation I stay at my grandmother's house. Her excellent meals consist of the tastiest food. My grandmother is a gourmet cook. Her cooking is tantalizing enough to make your mouth water even after you have eaten and feel full. I enjoy sitting in her cozy kitchen, watching her prepare a meal.

She stands by the stove with an apron tied around her waist, a spoon in one hand and a loving cheerful look on her face. The dishes that are the result of her work are more than perfect. She fries the fish to a perfect shade of golden brown. Her pancakes are round and even; they never burn. Her burgers are flipped with an expert flick of her wrist, resulting in a chorus of sizzles. Her meat is never too tough or too soft and her soups never boil out. Her eggs are perfect and her mashed potatoes aren't lumpy.

I could go on about all the food my grandmother makes. In short, the variety and abundance of food that my grandmother makes can sustain our entire family for days.

Shiffy Z.

❦

I picture my grandmother standing in her kitchen. She is wearing an apron tied around her waist and flowered slippers on her feet. Her specialty was making chocolate roll cake (kokosh cake). She would make ten rolls at a time and give them out to all her grandchildren. My family always looked forward to the three rolls of fresh chocolate roll cake we received. My grandmother had a special touch. We would freeze the cake and within the next few days there was not a crumb left.

Similarly, I remember how excited I was to go to my grandmother on a Sunday afternoon to bake with her. I would sit on a chair in her kitchen and watch her carefully make the cakes. After I watched her do it step by step I was able to make my own cake. I would roll out the dough with a rolling pin and smear on the chocolate. I remember feeling so proud when my grandmother took my hot fresh cakes out of the oven.

A grandmother's cooking has an extraordinary taste. She seems to add a special ingredient. Nothing anyone else will make can be the same. My grandmother's chocolate roll cake had a good taste that no other cake can duplicate. When I try to make the same cake it is never quite the same.

Rivkie F.

❦

*W*e usually hear about grandmothers who make the best honey cake and the fluffiest knaidels. They can make the perfect challah and the tastiest chicken soup. On the other hand, my grandmother makes the best sugarless challah and super saltless soup. My grandfather loves her cooking but I don't. My grandfather can't have sugar and my grandmother doesn't eat salt. I love my grandparents but I usually don't like their food. My mother says I have to learn to appreciate it.

So I try. If the soup isn't so spicy, I tell myself that the main thing is the love my grandmother put into it. If the rugalach seem a bit bland I tell myself it's only food. My grandmother's cooking teaches me to appreciate what I have. When I go to my grandparents I just grin and appreciate what I have — a grandfather and grandmother.

Sara G.

⌘

✦ Chicken Soup

*E*very Friday night we eat at my grandmother's house. Her specialty is chicken soup. Everyone enjoys it. It's the best chicken soup in the universe.

Every Friday afternoon my grandfather goes to the market. He buys carrots, celery, parsley and chicken bones. He brings them home to my grandmother. He watches as she cuts, peels and adds ingredients to create the best chicken soup in the universe.

One Friday night we sat by the table and my grandmother looked a little dazed. We didn't say anything. When I tasted the soup I knew that something was wrong. But I didn't say anything.

As my grandmother walked us to the door she told my mother, "My sweetest, next time please bring the children."

My mother was surprised. "The children are right here," she replied.

My grandmother lifted my chin and said, "This isn't the Chavie I know. My Chavie is a baby."

My mother took my hand and we walked to the steps. I looked up and noticed tears on my mother's face.

"What's the matter? Is grandmother sick?" I asked.

"Yes, dear. Bubby has Alzheimer's."

"Will she get better?"

"I'm afraid she'll get worse," my mother replied. "However, we still have to come and visit. That's what family is for."

We continue to visit every Friday night. On a better day my grandmother can cook, but sometimes my grandfather makes the soup. The soup is not the same but it is still delicious. Often, I still ask for doubles.

Rikki B.

❦

❧ *Grandmother's Cooking*

*M*y grandmother helps special children every day. She cooks for the orphans at an orphanage.

The actual cooking is rather hard for her. She is stuck in a small room in the basement with no air. In the summer there is no air conditioner, and all the ovens are on. In the winter there is no heat. The basement is the coldest part of the building.

Don't you enjoy the freedom of taking a second helping or going to the refrigerator to have an apple? In this home the food is limited. It seems that there is never enough. The children come to my grandmother for doubles and triples. She refuses with a heavy heart. She feels bad, but she has no choice. She has asked for a bigger supply of food for the children but was refused.

The children run into the kitchen to steal food. This can be annoying while you are trying to cook. They can get aggressive. I once went to visit and got frightened by a group of these children. I ran away. In the meantime I saw my grandmother handling the situation very well. She is so gentle and loving.

I realized then that these children are real people. I went back in without any fear. I just felt a strong feeling of love.

Mimi S.

❦

*O*ver the course of our lives we all encounter terrific people. These people leave a profound mark on our lives. I have been extremely fortunate. I can meet these people on a daily basis.

There is something deeply satisfying about walking into the kitchen and finding freshly baked cookies that your grandmother has sent.

I look forward to Friday. On Friday I go over to my grandmother's house. When I arrive I'm greeted by a warm welcome. My grandmother constantly urges me to sit down and eat something. I see the freshly baked challah or the cake just out of the oven and it already feels like Shabbos.

There is nothing quite as comforting as sitting down with your grandmother and sampling a morsel of her newest recipe. We catch up on the week's events. She tells me stories of how she lived in Europe as a young girl and reminisces about how different life was back then compared to our life now.

My grandmother is utterly amazing. She always reacts to a hard situation in a positive manner. She remains calm whether faced with easy or difficult situations. She is considerate, helping people in need. I respect her.

My weekly Friday visits aren't just wonderful because of my grandmother's cooking. There are life-long lessons that come along with it. These visits will remain with me throughout my life.

Esty R.

૭૦૯

Family is a precious gift. These are the people in our lives who give us many precious, intangible gifts. The value of these gifts cannot be weighed or measured. We look to our parents and grandparents for a helping hand, a hug, a smile and a look of understanding. They bring out the best in us and take the time to listen to us. They understand our problems and our conflicts. From a perspective of experience they can offer us wisdom.

Our younger siblings also teach us important life lessons as well. A young child has a different perspective. She thinks you are the greatest person in the universe. Those little running footsteps and that smile of delight that your baby sister or brother greets you with makes you forget every problem. For your toddler sibling, life is new and fun. Their innocent words of wisdom are often remembered for a long time.

❧

❧ *That Precious First Moment*

*G*ifts *are great. Surprise gifts are even more exciting. What comes to your mind when you hear the word "gift"? Probably you are thinking of a big box. It is covered with gift-wrap and has a pink bow on top. Of course there is a present inside. Sometimes it is a set of sefarim, a beautiful leather siddur or a dazzling piece of jewelry. Presents come in many colors, shapes and sizes. Once I received a gift that was the best ever, and it didn't come in a box.*

It was Motza'ei Shabbos and I was in camp. We were preparing for a big night of singing and dancing. Suddenly I heard the announcement that there was a phone call for me. I picked up the receiver and heard my mother's voice. "Mazel tov! You have a new baby brother!" she shouted into the phone.

"What? A baby? Mazel tov," I replied. I was surprised. My mother had told me that the baby was expected after the summer. It was a pleasant surprise and a wonderful gift from Hashem. My brother is a miracle!

Rivkah S.

❧

When we reminisce it helps make us aware and reminds us that this precious someone in our lives is a gift. When a cute baby grows up we sometimes forget how treasured that first moment was when we received this priceless gift. At the core of our life is a tremendous love for our sibling. Yet a reminder of that precious first moment helps us smile at them now. Now, when they are holding our favorite music tape and rapidly pulling out the long brown metallic threadlike component from the white plastic case, remember the gift so that anger won't take over and make you forget.

∽◈∾

◈ Of Rosy Cheeks and Wide Eyes

*L*ife flies by like a dream. Isn't it mind-boggling that once upon a time you didn't mind wearing your shoes on the wrong feet? Children are such happy human beings. Yet they possess such heartwarming sensitivity and innocence.

Children. They are the ones who stomp in muddy puddles and sing off key. They give you sticky kisses and hugs for no reason. Why is it that they can forgive and forget so easily? How is it that they are able to live most of their dreams? Kids are so sensitive only because they haven't yet learned how not to care. Children are honest with themselves. They are also so naïve and believing.

For all these reasons young ones have the ability to inspire others. One such example occurred several weeks ago when someone was staying at our house. He had been going through a tough period in his life and the following episode about my younger brother was an inspiration to him.

Several weeks before, my mother walked home with Chaim from his kindergarten orientation. It was a humid, hot, sticky day and Chaim was licking his ices, deep in thought. They were close to home when he stopped eating and looked up with a start. He had left his arts-and-crafts project at school. My mother was too tired to walk back. She asked him, "Are you upset?" Chaim hesitated. Then with a sparkle in his eye he announced, "You know, Mommy, there was once a man named Nachum Ish Gam Zu and whenever he lost something, he said 'Gam zu l'tovah!' This is also for the best."

There must be times when we all wish we could be kids again. Children are the ones whose tears we sometimes laugh at and whose smiles make us cry.

Shevi G.

༄༅

❧ Two Baked Apples

I pricked the apple several times and put it on a plastic plate. After reaching for the sugar shaker I turned it over and shook it twice. I set the dial on the microwave for five minutes, placed the apple inside and waited for the signal.

The plate was steaming. I reached for a spoon, mumbled a blessing and began eating. One spoonful followed another. As I ate each spoonful my mind wandered. I reviewed a list of things to do. Worries, problems and challenges rose in my consciousness. My mind was miles away from the apple before me.

My great-nephew began to "talk" in a complaining tone. He pointed to the apple. I took another apple, pricked it a few times and popped it into the microwave. The bell rang. The apple was ready. I placed it in the freezer so it would cool off quickly.

I sat down opposite my great-nephew and fed him a spoonful of the apple. He can't speak yet but he smiled. I gave him a second spoonful of the apple. He showed his eight white teeth. I lifted the spoon again. He giggled with appreciation. At the fourth serving he lifted his hands. For the fifth spoonful, he gurgled. I looked into his happy brown eyes and felt my stress melt away.

This simple apple means so much to him. He has such a pure soul. He's young enough to find delight in life's small gifts.

I said the blessing after food aloud for both of us with a happy grateful heart.

༄༅

*D*id you ever wonder how a six-pound baby has 248 limbs, 365 sinews and a vast amount of blood vessels coursing through his tiny body? Even some of the most educated scientists have come to the realization that the miracle of life is something only G-d can provide.

Often when a baby is born there are so many practical things that must be attended to that we don't take time to realize this miracle. There is the house to tend to, the infant's constant crying for his needs, and of course a simchah to be organized.

My mother recounts how one of her rebbetzins from way back gave the following advice:

"Dance with your baby at least once a day."

Her message is to rejoice. Sing, dance and feel happy in your heart for the spark of life you have been blessed with.

Chava Esther O.

❧ *Miracle on the Highway*

*E*arly in the morning we set out on our trip to Shop-Rite. Sheets of rain were pelting our windshield. The wipers were furiously pushing aside the rain, giving us a clearer vision of the road. The road was winding with sharp turns in spots. On our right we noticed a big red sports car, radio blaring. The driver behind the wheel was young and husky. I was frightened when I glanced his way, but I didn't know why.

Suddenly the red sports car skidded and crashed into our car with a tremendous bang. I heard my mother screaming out the names of each of her children. I jumped out and my mother pulled my siblings out of the car. We were all unharmed, baruch Hashem.

My younger brother is 5 and he seemed frightened by the ordeal. "Mommy," he asked innocently, "before we left this morning, you asked me if I davened. I did. But ... did you? My teacher said we must always pray every morning."

The message was clear to us. No one will ever know why the accident happened. However, the innocent remark of a 5 year old penetrated our hearts and remained there forever.

Chany G.

Gathered Around the Table

Gathered around the table
We survey a splendid scene —
On the hand-embroidered tablecloth
Crystal glitters, silver sparkles near gleaming china trimmed with gold.

Gathered around the table
Which dish do I sample first?
The colorful vegetable display
Or the famous mocha cheesecake with the almond border?

Gathered around the table
Waiting for the soup
A closeness between cousins surfaces
We feel serene, calm and complete.

Gathered around the table
We marvel at the perfect *latkes*
And admire eight tiny lights
Reflected on a frosty windowpane.

Gathered around the table
Laughing at a toddler's precocious comment
Celebrating our family's growth
Wondering how it happened so fast.

Gathered around the table
The main course is served,
We savor Grandmother's famous cooking
And a lively song begins.

Gathered around the table
Passing the empty plates to the corner
Where they are neatly stacked
And waiting for the dishwasher.

Gathered around the table
Grabbing cameras and snapping pictures —
Trying to hold onto the moment
That has already become a hazy memory.

❧ Family Time

*I*n these turbulent times every ordinary day is a special gift. One Shabbos, I sat at the table and decided to enjoy this family time. The table was laden with the special delicious Shabbos foods. Just looking at it sent a warm feeling up my spine. Of course the family sitting around the table dressed in their most beautiful Shabbos attire adds to the feeling of specialness and contentment.

It was an ordinary scene, yet it was so magnificent. My brother-in-law's soothing voice singing zemiros seemed to soar straight from his heart up to the Kisei HaKavod. My adorable 2-year-old nephew was sitting on his lap, trying to sing along while his little brother clapped from his perch in the high chair. How cute they looked. All was harmoniously peaceful in my home. My heart soared with gratitude during this beautiful moment.

The times we live in are unpredictable. Accidents, terror and torment have become the day-to-day norm. Perhaps if we take the time to think about and thank Hashem for our families and all the uneventful yet beautiful moments in our lives we will merit His yeshuah.

Fraydel Y.

❧ Can You Guess?

*T*he aroma of hot potato latkes filled the air. The tables were filled with cakes, cookies, fruit and other delicacies. The sounds of happy chatter echoed. My grandmother had prepared a Chanukah party in her home.

The children played dreidel with their cousins. We ate, sang and listened to Torah thoughts. Some of the cousins prepared a play to entertain the family.

The hightlight of the night arrived when we presented my grandmother with a huge Chanukah gift. My two cousins carried a tremendous box wrapped with paper and ribbons into the dining room. My grandmother looked on with interest.

We challenged my grandmother to guess what was in the box. Her curiosity peaked as she thought of what the box might contain. She made her way toward the box. She pulled at the strings and pried it open. Something jumped out at her.

"Happy Chanukah!" shouted her youngest grandchildren as they jumped out of the box.

My grandmother thanked us all. "This is the best gift you can give me."

Ruchy W.

❦

Phone Calls

In the United States there are thankfully no food lines. We don't have to line up and wait to buy bread, or coffee, or even chicken. However, every week during the summer, on Friday afternoon, I waited for two hours on line. I waited at the camp's public telephone to call and wish my parents a good Shabbos. This phone call was a privilege. Only the staff was permitted to make calls. As I stood there for two hours waiting my turn, I imagined my parents' surprised and delighted voices. I would speak for only 3 minutes, but it would be worth the wait. We wait when we care.

Sometimes I've sat waiting for the phone to ring. Sometimes I was worried. I longed to be standing right nearby. It's good to hear that familiar voice at such a time.

There are phone calls that have changed our lives forever — positively and negatively. We carry those moments with us every day of our lives. The message of the moment echoes in our mind. We even remember where we were standing, who was near us, and what we were wearing. We remember how our face broke into a smile. We think about the happy dazed expression and the joy that rose inside us. Those memories are important.

❦

Siblings are always there. They rejoice with you when you feel happy and encourage you when you feel sad.

✒ *Your Most Loyal Friend*

Someone to ease your pain,
Someone to play with in the rain,
She's the pillow that absorbs your tears —
A person who really cares.

Someone who won't hesitate to do a good deed,
She'll be your comfort in a time of need.
Someone who will keep her promise,
Someone you can depend on forever.

This same someone
Can also bother you all day long,
Upset you with her endless loud song.
Mess up all your stuff,

Annoy you when your day was tough.

This same someone
Has the ability to wreck your day;
Will borrow without asking first.
She'll ignore what you say,
Insist on having everything her way.

This same someone
May drive you crazy,
Make a mess, then be lazy.
She loves to pester night and day.
But come what may —
She is your best SISTER!

Leah O.

༄

It was Monday, January 24. All day long, I was waiting for the day to end. I wanted to be at home. At any moment something important could be happening, but here I was just sitting in class. Mrs. K., my English teacher, continued her lengthy mono-logue about Macbeth and his conflicts. I checked my watch — it was 3:20. I dreaded the hour and a half that I still had to remain in my seat. I checked my watch again. It was 3:22. I sighed.

Suddenly the intercom roared, "Is Reich in this class? Tell her to come to the office." Before the teacher could answer, I had already flown out the door.

I almost tripped on my own two feet as I ran down three flights of stairs to the office. I was greeted by a warm smile. "Mazel tov! Your mother had a baby boy. You can go home now."

I raced back up the three flights of stairs to class. Grabbing my books, I stammered the wonderful news to my friends. My friends were all happy for me. My legs couldn't carry me home quickly enough.

When I arrived home my aunt was there. My father took all of us to visit my mother in the hospital. I walked down the sparkling white hall and heard the echo of my footsteps. I could barely wait to see my newest brother.

I thank Hashem every day for the new addition to my family. But as for being the oldest of eight children — that's another story.

Chava Sheindel R.

The Gift
of Friendship

Although we think that friendship just happens, it's important to realize that we have to acquire friends. We need to treat others with patience and consideration. We can stop and think things over at the beginning of the day. We can ask ourselves, "What can I do to make a difference to someone whom I will meet today?"

We may think that friendships grow from dramatic or big events, but the fact is that the small considerate daily acts are what build a relationship. Think about your friend's feelings. Appreciate the good things she has done for you. Speak in a warm and upbeat tone of voice. When there is a problem that you want to discuss try not to do so in an annoyed tone of voice.

Sometimes you are there for a friend with a smile. Sometimes you are there with a listening ear. At other times you are there for your friend with an encouraging word or a compliment. For certain occasions you are there with a cake to share in her *simchah*. Most people wait for the other person to make the first move. However, *you* can choose to act first. Be a friend!

The Art of Making Friends

Make a list of the talents that contribute to our world. There are those who are musically gifted. They add so much to our lives with a symphony of instruments, song and harmony. Artistic aptitude creates beautiful surroundings. These gifts include paintings that we stand and admire, photographs that capture memories, or the perfect idea that pulls together all the parts of a room into a beautiful whole. Those who can run, swim, jump and play other sports well add fun and excitement to our lives. Of course before a test it's the organized scholar with the accurate notes that we seek. However, there is another talent that adds so much to our lives. It's the ability to connect with others.

Some people have a talent for knowing just the right thing to say. They are sensitive to the feelings of anger, despair, helplessness and sadness and also to the smile of accomplishment, triumph or delight. They help you share your experiences and express your feelings. At every gathering they make those around them feel safe and comfortable. Many great people were praised because of their ability to reach out and touch the lives of others.

Wherever you go today think of a way to spread joy to others.

R' Yochanan ben Zakkai lived at the end of the period of the Second Temple. He was the leader of the generation. His righteousness, prodigious memory, talent and depth of Torah knowledge cannot be fathomed. Yet Rabbi Yochanan is praised for always being the first to greet everyone he met. He greeted fellow Torah scholars first. Our Sages tell us that he also greeted young children first. He even greeted the gentile he passed in the marketplace first. This was R' Yochanan's strong point. It seems that it isn't such a simple matter. Perhaps we should develop this characteristic too.

Someone who can make people feel comfortable can accomplish a lot. It may seem like a small thing but it can have a big impact. Encouraging words may be remembered for years. One can definitely achieve more when one has help or support. Many lasting friendships begin with a pleasant greeting. Sometimes a small favor brings a significant benefit many years later.

How popular are you? It's a difficult question to answer. Does being popular mean that others run to greet you? Perhaps we can say that the truly popular person is the one who reaches out to others.

Meyer Birnbaum writes: "[In] the course of a lifetime, one meets two or three outstanding individuals who tower above everyone else. Mike Tress was one such person. One of the biggest shocks of my life was the week Mike was married. I wasn't invited, and I couldn't understand how he could have forgotten to invite his best friend. I mentioned this oversight to a few of my friends, and in each case the reaction was the same. 'What do you mean, you're his closest friend? I'm his closest friend.' None of us, unfortunately, could bring any definite proof — we had all been left off the guest list. Mike's magnetism was such that whenever you were near him he made you feel that you were the most important person in the world to him."

Reaching Out to Others — Quiz Yourself

Don't worry if this short quiz that follows indicates that reaching out to others is difficult for you. Most people will admit that this isn't their strong point. It's easier to wait for someone to come over to us and say something nice. We tend to worry about the reaction to our friendly overture. What if I'm not welcomed? What if she just stares silently? What will I say next?

It's so easy to rationalize instead of being friendly. We tell ourselves: she's probably not interested, or she has other friends, or she's not my type.

Give yourself 5 minutes for the following exercise. Read each sentence. Take a deep breath, then check the selection that matches how often you feel or act this way. Remember that you can always begin *now* to see things in a new way.

1. I find it difficult to say "Hello" to someone who is lonely.
   a) always   b) often   c) sometimes   d) rarely/never

2. When I do say "Hello," I say it hurriedly and walk away.
   a) always   b) often   c) sometimes   d) rarely/never

3. I feel awkward when I'm asked to work with someone new on a class project.
   a) always   b) often   c) sometimes   d) rarely/never

4. I always sit with my close friends, because I want to be liked.
   a) always   b) often   c) sometimes   d) rarely/never

5. When making plans with friends, I tend to agree with whatever they suggest that we do.
   a) always   b) often   c) sometimes   d) rarely/never

❧

I know a girl who does an unbelievable amount of chesed. Very few people know about these kind acts. She started it in elementary school and she still continues although she is about to graduate high school. There are some girls in the class who have very few friends. Perhaps it's because they look different or are shy. It could be that they are scholastically on a lower level although they are our age. If you are friendly with them the other girls look at you differently. Yet at every break this girl is friendly to these members of the class. She is not concerned about what others may think. She keeps in touch when the girls aren't in school. If not for her, they often wouldn't have anyone to talk to. Baruch Hashem they have her as a friend. I'm glad she's my friend, too.

Leba M.

❧

Do not be afraid to make overtures to "less popular" classmates. Do not worry about what others will think. It's more important to do what is right. The one who can be a friend to others will have true friends too.

Having friends who are happy for you is great. Some friends are naturally demonstrative, warm and kind. They don't hesitate to run over and greet you with a smile and a hug. Others are more reserved and feel more comfortable giving a compliment or writing a note. It's nice when your friends take the time to call you.

There are different forms of friendship and each has its place. Really close friendships are few and far between. Remember that they should be treasured.

A friend can show she cares about you in many different ways. For example, she can wait for you at the corner or save a seat for you in the lunchroom. You feel a warm glow when a friend shares her sandwich because you forgot to bring lunch. Perhaps your friend is eating a chocolate bar and she offers you a piece. Of course, there are much more serious situations in life which can also be a time for a show of friendship and support. These may include illness, family problems and loss. True friends can be of crucial importance at such a time.

It is so wonderful when friends value your special qualities. Friendship is a two-way street. If you are there for your friend she will be there for you. A true friend is empathetic, considerate and loyal. You want to help each other, and share the good times and bad. Friendships are one of life's greatest gifts.

Friendly Spoonfuls

On a chilly winter day settle down for a chat with a close friend. Make cups of hot cocoa and stir with delicious candy-coated spoons (recipe below) to make the cocoa and conversation even sweeter.

You will need:

One cup of chocolate

White chocolate chips

Styrofoam cup

Metal spoon

Two new plastic spoons

Colored sugars, decorative candies, and sprinkles

Waxed paper
Scissors

Microwave the chips about 2 minutes or until melted. The chips will still look solid, so you will have to stir them with a metal spoon. Dip each plastic spoon in the melted chocolate. Leave the top half of the handle uncoated. Immediately press the spoon onto the colorful sprinkles and sugars. Place the spoons on waxed paper to set. It will take about half an hour.

●◆ Vice President

*B*oth phone lines were ringing without a stop until midnight. The same words were repeated over and over again. "Congratulations! We are so happy for you! We heard that you are the next vice president of the High School G.O."

Several friends came over with a big ice cream cake to celebrate, while others just called on the phone to express their happy thoughts for me.

This whole year is one that I will cherish. There are the obvious assignments of a vice president, and I want to do more. I look forward to working hard, going around to the classes, following up on important plans. Part of being vice president is to simply be a friend. When I'm extra nice and helpful to other girls they appreciate it. They feel special that someone who is part of the G.O. cares about them. I cherish the smile and the happy faces I see when I say and do things for others. I pray to Hashem for the wisdom and the strength to be a help to others.

Shani K.

೧๑൭

Shani asserts that there was an amazing amount of support and togetherness among her friends. They felt that her success was their success. They were happy for her and even organized a small surprise party to celebrate. It's beautiful when a girl can believe, "If my friend triumphs that is also *my* success." It's even more wonderful when girls actually help one another. There are countless ways to demonstrate your assistance. Perhaps you can recommend a friend for a job, share the work on a project, or be there to offer support in an emergency. Hopefully, such friendships will continue for Shani (and others) after graduation.

⌘

I am a marathon runner: full of energy, always moving and ready for the next challenge.

I am a mountain climber: Slowly but surely I am making my way to the top.

I am a banker: Others share their trust and values with me and never lose interest.

I am a millionaire: rich in love, sincerity and compassion. I won a wealth of knowledge, wisdom, experience and insight that is priceless.

Most important — I am me.

Amy Yerkes

⌘

How well do you know your friend?

Would she or wouldn't she:

Stand up to a bully?

☐ Yes　☐ No

Wait for you if you had to stay longer to finish your test so that you could walk home together?

☐ Yes　☐ No

Tell you honestly that your blouse doesn't match your skirt.

☐ Yes　☐ No

Keep a $20 bill in her purse for two weeks and ask every girl she meets if they lost money?

☐ Yes ☐ No

Let you borrow her notes before a test?

☐ Yes ☐ No

Help you wash the dishes because your mother said you can't leave until you finish this chore?

☐ Yes ☐ No

Be happy for you if you were elected vice president of the G.O?

☐ Yes ☐ No

Which does she like best?

Circle choices:

☐ CLOTHES — Starched shirt, striped polo, pleated skirt, anything black, denim skirt, white sweater, casual, dressy, solids or prints.

☐ SHOES — Nikes, penny loafers, black slip-ons, patent leather pumps, high or low heels.

☐ FOOD — Veggie burger, biscotti, pizza, sushi, tuna sandwich, butter bagel, Cajun fries, health food, junk food.

☐ ACCESSORIES — Baseball cap, wallet, sunglasses, watch with a square face, pocketbook with a bow, Burberry scarf, jewelry.

☐ SUBJECT — Writing, *hashkafah*, prayers, discussion, math, lunch.

☐ BOOKS — *parashah* stories, historical novels, biography, mystery.

❦

1. What are her favorite things to do on a Sunday?

_____

_____

_____

2. How does she spend her allowance?

_____

_____

_____

3. What does she find annoying?

_____

_____

_____

4. Whom does she enjoy visiting?

_____

_____

_____

5. What thing can't she manage without?

_____

_____

_____

6. What does she like best about you?

_____

_____

_____

Circle Her Dream:

1. Success:

    a) Mother

    b) Head of Bikur Cholim

    a) Principal of high school / teacher

    d) Professional – nurse, doctor, lawyer, P.T., O.T.

2. Best place to live:

    a) Hong Kong

    b) Florida

    c) Israel

    d) New York

3. Perfect night activity:

   a) Bake
   b) Paint
   c) Attend a concert
   d) Bike toward the sunset

In a nutshell:

_____

_____

_____

_____

_____

_____

When you do this exercise you may find that you and your friend have similar tastes. On the other hand, you may find that the two of you are different, and that is okay, too. Our differences make us interesting.

Nevertheless, there is an inner dimension that unites the two of you. Within each of you there is a holy spark that is :

   1. pure
   2. purposeful
   3. creative
   4. caring
   5. loving
   6. able to make wise choices
   7. grateful

When you keep this inner dimension in mind it is easier to go beyond limitations and differences. Our essential integrity overcomes our various disagreements. Don't allow yourself to be confined by little things. A friend lets you express yourself and still respects and appreciates the real you.

I cannot figure out what she was referring to. I glance around the room and sigh. The air is stuffy. It is hard to breathe. The wall in the back of the classroom is lined with pipes and the floor is made of bathroom tile. There are no windows in the room. When the steam rises the knocking in the pipes practically drowns out the teacher's voice. My mouth tastes like old apples and my nose fills with what smells like dirty socks. This room looks like an underground cellar.

I suddenly felt someone put her arm around me. Startled out of my reverie, I glanced up and realized that my classmates were singing. Within moments, I was swept up in the united song: "Hinei mah tov u'mah na'im ..." [How wonderful when we sit together with a feeling of closeness and brotherhood.]

After a few minutes I realized what my mother had referred to. There is no doubt in my mind that some of our classrooms were not planned by a modern architect (this one is obviously makeshift). However, the spirit inside is far more precious than a beautiful building on the outside. The wonderful lessons I learn here every day are a valuable treasure. The friendships I am forming and developing under this roof are cherished and priceless. I hope they will escort me on my journey through life.

Mindy F.

Mindy realized that her dull, repetitive days can be filled with joy. Yes, you might be squished into a small room, but on the other hand you are friends together. The atmosphere may be warm and stuffy but there is also the warmth of a friend's smile. The walls may need a paint job but that's good, because since they aren't fancy and new the school allows the students to decorate those walls. Some lessons are boring but your friends fascinate you. Instead of waiting for the bell to ring why not savor these moments of friendship and song?

School gives you the opportunity to connect with others. You can share ideas, stories, encouraging words and a smile with your friends. Discover your talents by working on projects with others. Realize what's really happening. Everything looks different when you appreciate the precious gifts of friendship that grow each day inside the classroom. Here is a fun project you might want to try. Prepare this to celebrate a friend's birthday, the end of midterms or another happy occasion.

Sweet Treat Pizza

When everyone is feeling hungry they reach for a favorite food. Pizza is one of those favorite foods. There are so many delicious varieties of pizza: with cheese, without, vegetables, etc. Here is an original one. Bake this with your friends and let them select the special candy bar toppings.

You will need:

2 mixing bowls and mixer
measuring cup
½ cup flour
½ teaspoon baking soda
¼ teaspoon salt
1¼ sticks margarine (softened)
½ cup sugar
½ cup brown sugar
1 egg
½ teaspoon vanilla extract
1 package of chocolate chips
cookie sheet
½ cup peanut butter
spoon
1 cup of your favorite candy bars, broken into tiny pieces

Preheat the oven to 375 degrees. In a small bowl, mix the flour, baking soda and salt and set aside. In the large bowl, beat the margarine, sugar and brown sugar until smooth. Beat in the egg and the vanilla extract. Slowly beat in the flour mixture. Stir in one cup of chocolate chips. Spread the batter on a lightly greased cookie sheet. Bake 20 minutes. Crust should be light brown.

Remove the cookie crust from the oven and sprinkle the rest of the chocolate chips over the crust. Drop the peanut butter by spoonfuls on the melting chips. Let this stand for 5 minutes. Use the back of your spoon to gently spread the chocolate and peanut butter mixture. Decorate with crumbled candy bars, cool, slice and serve.

❖ Isn't Taking Attendance a Waste of Time?

I wondered what to do during those few minutes when my teacher took attendance. I glanced around the classroom for some ideas. I saw some girls daydreaming, others were whispering to each other and a few were reviewing for class. What should I choose to do? I had a thought. I would do something completely different. I would listen to the attendance and jot down the names of the girls who were absent so that I could call them tonight.

I thought that a 3-minute phone call would be an easy way to be friendly. However, it actually took a lot of courage for me to pick up the receiver and make the calls.

After I completed my homework, I looked at my scrap of paper with the names on it. Sara Goter was the first name on the list.

"I have nothing in common with Sara," I thought. "She is so shy. I won't know what to say to her. I can't just talk about the weather. It's probably too late to call anyway.

"You are just making up excuses," I told myself. "You really should call her, even if all you speak about is the weather."

I made those calls last night. Yes, there were a few uncomfortable moments when there was complete silence because I couldn't think of anything to say, but once the conversation got started it proceeded smoothly. I think each girl was happy that I called. My decision to listen to the attendance and note the absences was a good way to use those few minutes. I made others feel special

T.L.

∽◦∾

✥ Surprise Party

*A*s part of a volunteer program, my sister was the assigned mentor for a girl who was not yet religious. Energetically, my sister did everything she could to build a relationship. They went on outings, got together on Shabbos and spoke on the phone at night. August 13 was drawing near and my sister decided to make a surprise birthday party for Natasha. While my sister prepared her surprise, Natasha was preparing a surprise as well.

As 2:00 drew near, preparations for the party intensified. The large folding table stood in the middle of the dining room covered by a shiny yellow tablecloth. A big smiley face drawn in the center of the tablecloth made everyone who entered smile too. Yellow streamers matched the yellow plates that had a black border. Large bowls of assorted candies were set up throughout the room. Everything was ready . My sister left to make a phone call.

"Hi, Natasha! How are you? I have a book that I wanted to show you. Perhaps you would want to borrow it. Can you please come over to see it?"

Several minutes later the doorbell rang. We turned off the lights and ran to hide under the table. Only the lit candles on the cake illuminated the room. My sister quickly ran to answer the door.

"Surprise!" ten girls chorused, as the birthday girl entered the room. Natasha opened her eyes wide, her face crinkled into a huge grin, matching the smile on the tablecloth. She sat down at the head of the table and the party began. The hours flew by and soon it was time for everyone to leave, yet Natasha lingered.

"Rivka, I have something important to tell you. Yesterday my mother and father surprised me. I've asked them so many times and they have finally agreed. They said yes! They said we can light candles and keep Shabbos like the rabbi explained to us. Thank you so much."

As Natasha's eyes radiated real joy, my sister's eyes filled with tears. Natasha had just given her the better gift.

Esty O.

✺

*W*hat makes a terrific friend? Is she a close friend? Does she do dramatic things to help others? Someone can be a wonderful friend because she has an encouraging word and a friendly smile. Remembering minute details and acting thoughtfully can have a big impact.

One summer day in camp I was feeling a bit homesick. A friend of mine came over and sat down beside me. She said, "I was just listening to this song. I remembered that it's your favorite song. Listen!" She put on the tape and we listened together. I felt uplifted because someone cared. She remembered my favorite song and shared it with me. She made me feel terrific.

We should all realize that a little detail can make someone's day. We can always find something in each person that makes them great. Let's look for ways to treat each other with thoughtfulness and respect.

Basha T. L.

~ * ~

*D*uring this past summer I worked as a counselor. My co-counselor was a year younger than me. At first I wasn't sure if we'd work well together but I was pleasantly surprised.

On the first morning, she greeted me with a smile and introduced herself. However, she didn't smile only on the first day. Every morning she greeted me and our campers with a cheerful "Good morning." She was helpful as well. Whenever a girl lost something she offered to search for it. Second graders misplace their things often, yet she didn't lose patience when something was lost once again. She was always cheerful and enthusiastic. The girls were buoyed by her attitude.

Throughout the month I admired her contagious happy attitude. She didn't complain about tedious work. She didn't grumble about running up and down all the steps. Some of the activities were pleasant and others were dull, but my co-counselor *participated in all of them. She was a real role model. I'm glad I got to know her well.*

Yehudis R.

⮜⮞

How Popular Are You?

You would never guess that she was once shy in high school. She rarely mentions her fears and difficulties. She is the mother who jogs into my parenting class, the hostess at the school dinner, the efficient legal assistant. She is confident and self-assured. However, it wasn't always this way. Here are some of the feelings the workshop participants shared.

- "I was the most unpopular kid in the class. I was the one who was never invited to parties."

- "I remember the extra-curricular functions. If there was a play or choir everyone went to try out, but the teachers chose whomever they wanted."

- "I met someone at our high-school reunion. She told me that when she went from eighth grade to ninth grade she was at an academic and social low. Suddenly in high school there was no time for asking questions. You took your notes and your tests. She came into the school with a few close friends, but suddenly they didn't accept her in the same way as before."

- "I think the 'in clique' had a nucleus of two or three girls and another six or seven girls floating on the outside hoping to get invited. For example, everyone was friendly with the good student before a test but they wouldn't necessarily remember to invite her on a Chol HaMoed outing."

If there were a magic pill you could take to make you popular and confident, would you buy it? You probably would answer yes, without thinking twice. Popularity is probably a big goal for you.

Chapter 14

The Gift of a Close Friend

The Art of Listening — An Important Component of Friendship

It was one of those weeknights. Shaindy sat at the kitchen table and thought about the work ahead of her. Actually there was so much to do that she didn't know what to do first. After finishing supper, Shaindy knew she should start doing homework immediately, but she felt tired before she began. Why were her eyes closing? What time was it anyway? She looked at her digital watch. It was just 7:36, she noted with surprise. She felt like it was 10 o'clock. Why did teachers give three hours of homework after a long day of school? Even if she started right away she wouldn't finish until

10:30. Well, if it's late anyway she might as well call a friend. "I'll talk for only 5 minutes," she promised herself. "Leah is always so optimistic. Her encouragement will motivate me to complete my homework quickly."

Shaindy dialed her friend Leah's number. As she pressed the buttons Shaindy thought, "I wonder if I could do it with my eyes closed." Instead of the usual, "Hi, Shaindy! What's up?" she heard her frustrated friend complaining in a low tone, "I'm so disappointed that our school trip was cancelled on Sunday just because the bus broke down. I even bought a new sweater especially for the trip."

What would be your response to Leah's statement if you were her friend? Some people think it's their job to solve their friend's problems. They want to give great advice, cheer their friends up when they feel down and step in and do things for them because they can do them better. This doesn't really work. Although your friend might tolerate this occasionally, the friendship may suffer when one person always takes charge.

There is a way to empower your friend and at the same time let her know that you care about her. It's important to really *listen* to your friend. On the ship of friendship, although it's important for your friend to feel that you are both in the same boat, she also needs to feel some control — that she's holding the rudder and steering. Don't be the one who *always* decides the direction your ship should take. We all try to listen a little but after a few minutes we are tempted to jump in with our own ideas. That's why listening quietly and really letting your friend express her feelings is so valuable and powerful. You may be surprised at the deep ideas a friend might share with you once she knows she can trust you. At times it may feel a little scary, but believe in your friend. She can come up with good solutions too.

When you interrupt a friend to offer advice, she might just walk away from you, shrug her shoulders and say, "You just don't understand." This indicates that she feels you are not really hearing what she is saying.

Shaindy said, "It is frustrating that the trip was cancelled."

Her friend continued to complain, "Couldn't they have used a more responsible bus company?" Without scolding, Shaindy said, "It sure is hard when plans fall through at the last minute."

Then Shaindy asked, "What do you think we should do?" Suddenly Leah was her cheerful self again. "It doesn't pay to gripe about it. Would you like to go for ice cream cones together after school tomorrow?"

Shaindy smiled. She just knew her friend would give her something sweet to anticipate. "Well, I'm going to look forward to that and now I'd better go finish my homework, even though I'm not looking forward to it."

"Oh, so you've already begun. I'm impressed."

"Actually the only thing I did so far was open my book and call you," Shaindy answered.

With a laugh the friends said good-bye.

When someone is given a chance to explain how she's feeling and then asked what she would like to do without being given any advice, she usually can overcome succumbing to pessimism and reach for something better. No one wants to be told how to do things. It makes a friend feel that you are looking down on her or that you think she's stupid. Obviously this is not your intention.

Five Principles of Listening

Here are five tips to help you listen attentively and let a friend know you really care about her.

Listen effectively.

Keep pace with your friend's feelings without trying to change her direction. Instead of worrying about what *you* will say, concentrate on being empathetic. Every person needs to feel that they have worth and that their feelings are valid. It is important to everyone that someone accepts them and cares about them. Every individual needs someone who is accepting and isn't trying to change her. You can fulfill this need by just listening without talking.

There is a joining together when one person listens silently. Giving your friend a chance to speak will help clarify her thinking.

    a. LISTEN with concentration.

    b. LISTEN to the feelings.

    c. LISTEN to the wishes.

    d. UNDERSTAND from your friend's viewpoint.

Trust your friend.

Your friend is smart and capable. That's why you chose her. You can offer your help, but don't try to take over and do everything for her. Given the opportunity, your friend can cope. Be kind and gentle, but let your friend take care of things for herself. She can specifically request what she may need you to do.

It's so good to feel capable and realize that someone recognizes our abilities. Sometimes we may feel overwhelmed. At those times the most considerate thing a friend can do is to trust us.

Accept your friend's feelings without judgment.

Don't try to change or correct your friend's feelings. Keep your focus on understanding. Let your friend's words be your starting place. Giving wise counsel may make you feel good, but listening quietly will make your friend feel better.

It's great to be able to say *"Gam zu l'tovah"* about your problems, but when you say it to your friend it sounds like you are indifferent or minimizing what she is feeling. No one wants someone telling them, "You shouldn't feel that way."

Keep quiet until your friend is finished.

When someone is talking from her heart, don't interrupt, even if you have a great idea. Just listen and let your friend express her feelings. Often, just talking about the problem out loud to someone who is sympathetic helps the person pull out of the negative loop. Simply talking about the situation can give one a clearer picture of what they have to do. However, once in a while you can repeat a key phrase to reassure your friend that you are paying attention. For example:

Your friend says, "I spent all week going to play tryouts. They had auditions four times. I didn't get a part. I'm so disappointed."

You could say, "That would be disappointing. After all the stress of waiting and trying out and getting your hopes up, you thought you'd get some part."

Don't say, "Well, I'm sure you'll get a part next year." That won't cheer your friend up; it will just make her feel that you don't understand.

Learn validating phrases and questions.

Use validating phrases to let your friend know that you are really listening and that you care. A few simple ones are: "Oh, wow," "Hmmm, that would be hard," "I think I might have felt the same way." Validating questions help your friend be creative. Then she can think of her own plan of action. Some of these are: "What happened?" "What did you do?" "What do you think you should do?" "Is there anything I can do to help?" Using these phrases and questions helps your friend feel capable of solving her own problems.

As you put these principles into practice, you will be pleasantly surprised at how much your relationship with your friends will improve and thrive.

Dear Shira,

It's been a while since I've seen you last, but the image of your ever-cheerful smile gives me courage to pull through each day. There are no words that can express my appreciation. You brought a ray of sunlight into my life. How can a simple thank-you compensate for all you've done for me?

I came to camp this summer expecting it to be like my past seven summers in camp. I expected to sit in solitude with no one to confer with but myself. Then you entered the bunkhouse, looked right at me and smiled. I knew my life wouldn't be the same again.

You looked past the scar on my face. You had the courage to recognize the real me. I remember all those conversations we had until the wee hours of the night. You discovered all that I had to offer. You discovered that I too have a mind and heart.

Tell your friends that they don't have to do anything difficult or special. They just have to be themselves. A little bit of kindness can make a big difference.

Your friend,
Tamara

❧ Someone Who Listens

Listening to a friend's sorrow eases half her pain. Listening attentively is a great kindness. It feels wonderful to know that one is being heard. Everyone likes to be recognized and feel that what they have to say is worthwhile.

Many times when a friend is upset about something, she just wants to get it off her chest. Often, once she is clearheaded she can think of her own solution. She doesn't necessarily need your opinion, she needs your ears.

My father is an excellent listener. Whenever one of us children comes home upset after a hard day we can count on my father to hear us out. He never interrupts with his own advice until the other person has finished speaking. When he does give advice it's valued because he has listened first.

Listening to others shows you respect them and acknowledge that they are special. It means you put yourself aside. Someone who listens is someone who cares.

Chava Esther O.

❧ Invisible

I opened the heavy glass door and entered the lobby. There were rows of couches and end tables. The fixtures had once been elegant. The carpet was of good quality, but it was wearing thin in several spots. The faded wallpaper had an elegant floral pattern. The dusty lampshades were perched on the large lamps balanced on the end tables. The windows were covered by dingy venetian blinds. The room had an orange hue.

I walked toward the receptionist's desk. The lobby was totally silent. I didn't hear any music or conversation. I smiled at the cheerful blond-haired receptionist and inquired, "I'm here to see Beatrice. What room is she in?"

The receptionist looked up, surprised. "Beatrice should be right here in her usual seat in the lobby. I saw her come down half an hour ago. She's sitting all the way at the end near the window."

Startled, I looked around the lobby and noticed that it was full of people. There were rows of elderly men and women sitting on the couches. Some sat with their hands in their laps staring straight ahead. Others were holding a book or a newspaper. No one moved or spoke.

I didn't hear a sound from these silent "invisible" bodies. They sat three feet apart from each other, yet not one individual intruded on his neighbor's solitude. Each person was withdrawn into his own private world. There were at least forty people in the room, yet there was no interaction. The room was silent.

Slowly, I walked down the aisle in search of Beatrice. I felt the "invisible" eyes following me and watching my movements. There was no smile or sneer or utterance. But I felt the silent eyes measuring my route, following my progress. I guess they were curious about whom I had come to visit. I heard the echo of my footsteps.

The nurse whispered, "She's the third to the last over there on the right." I approached Beatrice and smiled. She seemed to look right past me. In a cheerful voice I called out, "Good morning!"

She just sat there staring, not moving. It seemed that she hadn't heard, so I tried again, "Good morning, Beatrice. I'm Roiza Weinreich. I came to visit you." Beatrice blinked.

"I'm Roiza Weinreich. My daughter came to visit you last week. She has told me many wonderful things about you." Beatrice smiled. "So I came to meet you today as well."

In an attentive, eager voice she said, "Good morning! What did you say your name was?"

"Roiza," I repeated patiently. "I'm Roiza Weinreich."

Then a very wonderful thing happened. Beatrice came out of her daze and began talking to me. She seemed reborn and animated. I described my hobbies and Beatrice laughed. I told her about the school that my daughters attend. Two decades earlier Beatrice had been the principal in that school. She seemed young again as she shared some of her favorite stories from those days.

As we conversed I felt many eyes watching me. How I wished that I could visit each "invisible" individual in that room. I would have liked to show each one his worth and make him feel human again. Wouldn't it be wonderful to have a conversation with more than one person? If I only had time.

"Why must you sit there like that?" I thought. "Why can't you be friends with one another? Why not talk to each other? Read aloud. Play a game. You can still do so much for each other. You may be feeling weak, but you can be a part of the world around you."

Perhaps being in an institution takes away the ability to interact in healthy ways.

I walked out feeling dazed. Surely there are many "invisible" people I pass each day. I walk down the street and pass people I have met once or twice, but I feel that I'm too busy to stop and say hello. I ride the bus in silence. I walk past an office and don't stop to say hello to the secretary. I walk past the children playing on the block, but I don't stop to smile. Perhaps I could reach out and make a difference in someone's life every day if I did.

～☙ॐ～

☙ *She Sits Alone*

A girl sits alone, ignored and invisible. From her empty corner of the classroom she looks wistfully at her classmates. The laughing girls are huddled in tight groups, chattering excitedly during the lunch break. These girl have always seemed to have everything — friends, good looks, happiness. They have everything she wishes she had. They always seem so carefree, but they don't include her in their fun and games. They are mean and awful. That's what she always thought. Until now.

Today was different. She had decided that just for one day, she would regard her classmates with a new, positive perspective. She was tired of being an outcast, a hermit in the corner who always silently resented the girls and looked for their faults. Today she would make an effort to look for the good. Suddenly she realized that there were good things happening while she sulked.

One classmate helped another with her homework, another taught her friend the classwork she had missed, and a third classmate offered to run to the grocery for someone who had forgotten her lunch. Although these were little deeds, today they were magnified in the eyes of this friendless student. As she watched them, she marveled at the generous way each one gave of herself to help another.

Well, then, why am I sitting alone? she wondered. Slowly she recalled vague memories of her first days in the class. She remembered the girls who had tried to befriend her. She remembered tentative offers of help. One girl had offered to sit near her, another to show her around the school. She had shrugged them off then. As she continued to resist their advances her peers had given up. Later when she opened herself up to companionship there were no longer any offers. Instead she had grown angry and bitter. Now she would have to take the first step.

Now she realized the importance of judging everyone favorably. It wasn't too late to look for the good and to find a friend.

Ayala R.

❧

A spectrum of colors shines through every human being. One person's forte may be strength, and another's sharpness of mind. You can find unique gifts in every person. How can we make the best use of our talents? Is it by viewing others with envy or with affection?

Ironically, when we yearn for another person's lot we end up appreciating ourselves less. If we avoid causing any discomfort to others and feel overjoyed at their success it will be easier for us to be happy with our own talents. If we have affection for others we will be able to use our gifts to their utmost as well.

Ruchy W.

Empathy and Hashgachah

The following anecdote shows how R' Aryeh Levine, a principal in Yerushalayim, used his keen insight to love and care for the students of his school.

When the time came in the morning for the young children at Eitz Chaim in Jerusalem to enter the classroom for their daily lessons, R' Aryeh Levine would stand at the doorway or at a window, and he would study each small boy — to the puzzlement of the children, who did not understand his reason.

One day his son asked him, "Why do you always stand at the entrance waiting for the pupils, and then look at them so closely as they enter?"

"Come and stand with me and take a close look at them," said R' Aryeh. "What do you see?"

"It is quite interesting to watch them come in," his son commented. "You can see how eager they are to study Torah. There I saw a boy pushing ahead of another. He has a zest for learning. That one over there, though, is not at all anxious to enter. His mind is still on the games he was playing."

"I look at different things altogether," said R' Aryeh. "That child's pants are torn. This one's shoes are quite tattered and worn. That boy over there is definitely hungry; how will he be able to study?"

R' Levine then did all that he could to help those children who were needy. (*A Tzaddik in Our Time,* p. 319)

- How do we look at others?

- Do we look at them with a nurturing eye or with a critical eye?

- What are most of our conversations about?

- Are most of our words critical and demanding or caring and supportive?

- What were the last five things you said to your friend?

- Remember to stop and think before you speak — once spoken, words cannot be taken back.

∼∂∾

Best-laid Plans

One area that clearly demonstrates Hashem's providence is in the way friendships develop. Once I planned to be in the same bunk as my best friend in camp. We both entered identical lists in the box that said, "Choose whom you would like to be with." Two months before camp began we were assured that we were indeed in the same bunk. We talked about the different experiences we would share for weeks. However, on the first day of camp we realized that the bunks were arranged differently this year. Instead of twelve girls occupying one large room, the bunk occupied two rooms. Six girls were in bunk 12A and six were in bunk 12B. You guessed right — my best friend was in the other room. I shared a bunk bed with someone I had never met before. At first I was disappointed, but it was really a heaven-sent opportunity. I quickly discovered that the girl who slept above me was cheerful, enthusiastic and fun to be around. We are still friends today. When my friend and I were separated, at first I thought I had lost a friend, but actually I gained one.

I have never forgotten the first moment I walked into the dormitory in Eretz Yisrael. When one is thousands of miles away from home one looks forward to the comfort of sharing a room with a high school friend. I had thought we could choose our roommates. I found out, however, that roommates are selected by a lottery. All my other friends from New York were together. I had two roommates. Someone came up to me and said, "Surprise! You have two roommates, one is from Chicago and one is from a small town in Israel." I probably felt traumatized for a few minutes.

Then my new roommate from Chicago entered. She looked vaguely familiar. We exchanged names. "I didn't recognize you, but this is *hashgachah pratis,*" she exclaimed. We had met at the Bais Yaakov convention and had exchanged addresses. Since then we were pen pals. It wasn't the way I had planned it, but I did have a close friend to be with this year.

Sometimes friends are supposed to be together. Other times we are thrown together with new people. When things don't go as we planned it's important to remember that there is a Planner in

Heaven guiding our steps. Often when we look back, we see clearly that His plan was the best thing that could have happened.

❧☙

❧ *The Letter*

*T*he memory of that fateful summer day is imprinted in my mind and it won't be easily erased. On that day the shield of childhood innocence began to crack. On that day I received the letter.

It was an ordinary letter from my dear friend Henny. It told of the usual summer activities in lovely scenic surroundings. Then I read those last four troublesome sentences.

"They're taking me out of your class. They don't care what we think about it. It's final and nothing will help. There's nothing we can do to reverse their decision."

I was horrified. It must be a joke. This can't be happening. I re-read it over and over again. I ran to my sister at the other end of the campus. I tried to hold back my tears. I thrust the letter in front of her and told her to read it. She looked at me and read the letter. When she finished, she gave me a big hug. "Hashem does everything for the best," she said. "It must be good somehow. Try to think rationally. Try to think like a grown-up."

"I am a grown-up," I yelled back. "You don't understand. You're just like the others. No one understands. The only one who understands is my friend Henny. That's why we're friends. How could they be so cruel? What are they trying to do?"

I flew out of the door before she could say another word.

The last week of the summer I was miserable. Most of my time was spent sulking or writing in my diary. I wondered what the new school year would bring. I dreaded that first day of school.

On the first day of school my fear became reality. My friend and I were in two different classes.

However, we were not split. Through it all, I learned that nothing can separate sincere friends. It did not matter if we

Like a ray of sunshine which guides, warms, and protects,
Like a drop of dew which sustains and refreshes,
A smile renews the vigor of the soul.

Sharing During Tough Times

We all dread needing help. We hate the vulnerable needy feeling. If we have to ask for help it's much easier when our parents are nearby. Yet sometimes we must face hurdles on our own. We have no choice and we have to turn to our friends for help. This is when we realize that there are friends and then there are FRIENDS.

Many friends will share their cookies, but only one friend will make sure to take a portion of every course that's served and save it for you under a covered plate because you were delayed. This considerate friend made sure that you didn't miss lunch. Many friends will be there when you open a box that came via UPS from home, but only one friend will surprise you with a snack she bought for you at the canteen. Many friends will borrow your stamps, blow dryer and money, but one friend will run up with a quarter when she sees you dropped yours at the public phone. Many friends will laugh at your jokes, but only one friend will listen to your aches. That friend is the one who ran over when she saw that you were hurt. Many friends will race you to the next activity, but this friend lends you her shoulder as you limp to the infirmary.

Are you a FRIEND? When someone is hurt do you notice and look away or do you set aside the time to look her way?

❧ A Friend's Comfort

On the second day of camp I got a second-degree burn on my hand. I was in a lot of pain. One of my friends kindly walked over to me and said, "B.T., my hand is also burning." This was a great comfort to me. My friend didn't realize that with just one sentence she took away half of my pain. Often when we see the pain of another we shrug and think, "Someone else will help." We don't realize the importance of our own comforting words or actions. By simply caring we can bring relief.

Basha T.

∽∂∾

*A*s the summer approached I felt the butterflies in my stomach acutely. I was filled with dread about going to a new camp. I hardly knew anyone. How would I manage to find a friend? What if I had an awful experience?

Then I met Blimi. Blimi was my counselor. She melted my fears. She escorted me to the bunkhouse, guided me around camp and introduced me to the other campers. At night she came to my room and asked how the day went. This occurred almost every night. She'd come in and we would talk until way past curfew. We shared our hurts, doubts, fears, joys and hopes. Although she was just three years older than I, she acted like a mature adult and treated me like one, too. Within a few weeks we became very close friends.

This past summer she was my supervisor and I was a counselor. Again our late night talks continued. Once the topic turned to relatives. I have an uncommon name so she inquired whom I was named after. I told her about it. She bolted upright. In a dazed manner she said that she was related to that person, too! It was great finding out that I was somehow related to someone whom I admire a great deal.

Machly Z.

∽∂∾

*T*he sun was shining brightly on the beautiful summer day. Most of the children were at the swimming pool. My sister, the lifeguard, had been roasting in the hot sun since early in the *morning. Everyone was uncomfortable in the 100-degree weather, and therefore no one paused to think about my sister's discomfort. However, one girl, Brochie, did notice.*

She's 18, but she has probably done more kindness than many people twice her age. With a wide smile, she came over to my sister and offered to take over her post for 10 minutes. "Go in, Hadassa, get wet, cool off and then come back. It's really no big deal."

This small act impressed me so much. She offered to watch the pool, but what was greater was her sensitivity. She noticed my sister and realized that she must be feeling uncomfortably hot, so she did something about it.

Esty O.

~∂∽

Demonstrating consideration is one of the ways you can express friendship. Showing a friend that you care means so much. A thoughtful action or remark can make a difference, so get in the habit. You will both feel better.

❧ *What Can I Say?*

My eyes were misty and my hands trembled as we spoke. My friend's mother had gotten very sick during the previous year. In the past few months her condition became critical. We said Tehillim. We mentioned her name in Shemoneh Esrei. Sometimes we heard that things were going better and we sighed with relief. Then there were the emergency days when the entire group took out some time to pray together. Most of the time, however, our life just went on.

My friend attempted to hide her emotions. I think it was hard for her to have to always pretend that she was the same person now that she had been beforehand. As a result, she became bitter and angry at the world. After a while, she opened up to me.

My friend often shared her fears and worries with me. She would tap me lightly on the shoulder and just begin telling me about the little things that were different. "Yesterday someone on the block brought supper for us. It was chicken again. We had chicken four times this week." I knew it wasn't the chicken that was bothering her, but I didn't know what to say.

I'd ask a simple question, "How are you?" My friend thrust her report card in front of me and asked, "Can you tell that it's my mother's signature?"

I looked at the report card. The first-term signature was bold and confident. The signature now at the end of the year was light and wavy; each letter seemed to have zig-zags. I know that when I said, "Sure. It looks perfectly clear," that I said it too loudly.

I was only in the eighth grade and I didn't know how to react or what to answer. Most of the time, I simply kept quiet, and offered a "listening ear."

I was standing and davening on Rosh Chodesh Elul. My friend whispered into my ear, "Yehudis, it's okay, you can now stop praying for my mother. It's all over." I gasped and continued to pray a hurried yet emotional Shemoneh Esrei. As I finished, I turned around and saw the rest of my bunkmates leaning on each other for moral support. Their red-rimmed eyes mirrored their anguish. I couldn't handle it anymore and I burst out crying on my friend's shoulder.

Someone came over and whispered, "Don't worry, it will be okay."

"No, it won't!" I cried out. "How can you say that? From this moment until the coming of Mashiach our friend will be an orphan. Everyone else can forget this terrible nightmare, but she will be living it."

My friend came to tell me good-bye. I felt so helpless. Here I was crying over her mother's death while she just stood there as strong as a brick wall. Yet I knew her well and I was able to see behind the wall to the real her. I saw a river of tears being shed from within.

"There's nothing I can do," I thought. I wish I had done more while her mother was alive. The silence was so thick between us. I knew I wanted to say something, but what could I say?

"Hashem, help me. Please give me the words to say to comfort her." I turned to my friend and said a few words. All I said was, "Shaindy, I love you and don't worry because I'm always here for you." That did it. She broke down and gave me a tight hug. We both cried on each other's shoulders.

The task of comforting a friend and sharing her pain may seem like a difficult ordeal for you to handle but to the person in need it may mean the world.

Yehudis W.

❦

*M*y grandmother wouldn't let a day go by without caring for another person. My grandmother stopped to smile at the old ladies whom everyone else passed without a glance. She would help those in need.

On a warm breezy day in Jerusalem, years ago, my grandmother moved her furniture out of her house into the large courtyard. She took everything out, from books to beds. My mother arrived home from school and was quite surprised to see the furniture in the yard. As she entered the house the delicious aroma of baking cakes drifted to her nose. My grandmother greeted her lovingly and explained, "There are two orphans who are getting married today. They aren't able to pay for a hall and a catered meal so I decided to make the wedding for them right here."

My mother smiled. She understood that this was another of her mother's daily acts of kindness. My grandmother also shared the pain of others. She didn't just stand by and sigh, leaving the toil of helping to others. She went to work right away.

Miss Lieman

Good Friends and Great People

Helping the developmentally delayed is definitely a kind thing to do. It's very important that these innocent children who talk and walk more slowly receive genuine love. One can truly make a difference. It's not this child's fault that she was born with a handicap and surely she should be embraced and not ignored. Those who volunteer for this essential and thoughtful work possess a unique blend of kindness, courage and enthusiasm. So many people will say, "It's a great thing to do but it's not for me."

Think about the last time you met someone who was "special." You might have been at the supermarket, a wedding or a concert. Perhaps your classmate was walking a special child to Bnos Chavivos. Did you pretend the special person was invisible? Did you talk only to your friend? Perhaps you felt guilty so you said a quick "Good Shabbos." After all, what could you say? How do you have a serious conversation with a special child?

Ruchy's view is very different. It may be hard work but it's worthwhile. She is comfortable and enthusiastic with her special friends. Not only does she take time each week to visit Mishkon, she looks forward to these encounters. She shares an inside view of her volunteer work. Ruchy emphasizes that she has discovered tremendous benefits in mingling with special children. These children are an inspiration and their companionship is enjoyable. They are not only her good friends, they are great people.

☛ *Precious Moments*

I look forward to the precious moments I share with my friends at Mishkon, a home for the developmentally delayed. I enjoy working with special adults and children because of their loving natures and the rewarding feeling that I get.

I feel successful when I learn and play with these special children. It takes a lot of patience to sit with them and to struggle to teach them something new. They put forth a lot of effort to grasp what I am telling them. It's worth all the struggling and countless mistakes to see their eyes light up when they finally figure it out.

One Sunday afternoon I was spending some time with Chana, a cute 8-year-old with Down syndrome. She told me how good I looked, to which I responded, "Stop, I'm blushing!" She caught on to the phrase. Now, every time she is complimented she sweetly replies, "Stop, I'm blushing!"

I was reading an article in a local newspaper about Mishkon. I was ecstatic to read a section in the article about Chana. The reporter had complimented her pretty dress. She proudly exclaimed, "Stop, I'm blushing!" Seeing those words in black and white made me feel proud.

The love at Mishkon is unsurpassable. These children love you and each other. Their love is unconditional. They are very devoted to those they learn to trust. They would never betray a friend. Every time I come, I am greeted with a shower of hugs and kisses. If I'm ever feeling down I go to Mishkon to be cheered up. Just to see their warm smiles helps brighten my day. They perceive when I'm not myself and strive to cheer me up. When it is time to leave I feel sad, but I already anticipate the next visit.

Mishkon is my favorite place to spend my free time. It feels great to feel loved and appreciated. I hope I will be able to continue these visits even after I have a family of my own. They are truly special and I will always cherish the time I spend there.

Ruchy Stauber

How do you have a serious conversation with a special child?

- Be patient
- Speak slowly
- Be willing to say things more than once
- Speak naturally and honestly

*S*hira Gross was born hard of hearing. With the help of hearing aids, sign language and lip-reading, she is able to communicate fairly well. Her speech, however, is somewhat slurred and unclear. Although she has a few good friends, many people treat her as an outcast because of her handicap.

I was at a hotel when I first met Shira. I was bored, lonely, and looking for someone to talk to. Behind me, I overheard someone talking in a different way. I was nervous to turn around. What would the owner of this unclear speech look like? I envisioned many different people of bizarre appearance in my mind before slowly turning my head.

What I saw when I turned around drastically changed my view of handicapped individuals. I saw a lovely tall girl with short dark hair and pretty shining eyes looking back at me and smiling. Shira has a heart of gold, and I enjoyed spending time with her.

Adina B.

❧

*S*omeone I know had her arm severed by an accident while standing at the corner waiting to cross the street. She often remarks that she is grateful that she is still alive. What if her head had been injured instead? She is married and has children. Once she visited my friend on Shabbos. My friend Tillie watched her diaper her baby with one arm. She asked, "How do you manage?" With a smile on her face she replied, "Tillie, how do you manage? Everyone has a handicap whether it is visible or not. Mine is physical so you can see it. Others may have a handicap that you cannot see." What a great life lesson!

If we take the time to become acquainted with someone who is handicapped we find out how special they really are.

Yosefa Bajnon

❧

Be a friend. Don't look at differences; look at the things you have in common. Don't look at her flaws; look at her assets and how to bring out the best in your friend. Smile — with your eyes, not just with your mouth. Be supportive and nurturing.

A friend isn't someone with whom you simply chatter. With a friend you can have a real conversation. Friends share hurts, fears, joys and hopes. Listen from the heart. Share your feelings. Be there during tough times.

It is better to find a few true friends than to be part of the "in group." A significant talent is the ability to be caring, sensitive and giving. Be loyal to your friends but at the same time try to meet new people too.

A small detail can make someone's day. Look for ways to be thoughtful. Treat everyone you meet with respect. Be the first to reach out to others. Don't wait! Friendship is a gift to be treasured.

The Gift of
Surmounting
Challenges

The stories in this book were written by real people. They are fact, not fiction. You've met girls who have achieved some wonderful accomplishments. I hope that you learned an important lesson so far — You can do it too!

Everyone dreams of becoming great. Everyone yearns for moments of triumph. Where are we looking for triumph? Do we want to get an important job, become famous, hear thousands applaud us or win a game? Do we dream of being the best? Achieving a goal that many people want and only few attain is one way to define success.

However, in this chapter you will meet people who have achieved a different type of success. When one lives life fully in spite of a handicap, one has triumphed. Someone who makes a difference with her acts of kindness is a success. If you quietly do something to help someone who really needs you, you have done a great feat. If you take a difficult circumstance and change it for the better patiently and quietly, you have conquered.

Each of us has an opportunity to change the world for the better. We can each plant a seed of kindness and spread some joy right where we are. That will make all the difference.

*L*ife isn't easy. Life isn't meant to be easy. Our life's purpose is to overcome obstacles and become better people. If life would be full of bliss we wouldn't feel a need to move on and up the ladder.

When faced with a difficult situation it takes willpower not to be dragged down. The point is not to complain or fall apart and give up. There is a benefit to every trial. There is something more than heartache that can be gained.

Every situation grants us experience and a lesson. However, the main thing to remember is: Grow from the situation. Overcome the situation and don't let it overcome you.

Basya D.

❧

❧ September 11, 2001

*O*n the morning of September 11, my father went to work as usual on the 77th floor of the North Tower of the World Trade Center. He was on the phone with my grandmother when he heard a terrible crash. The first plane had struck his building. He had experienced the 1993 bombing of the World Trade Center and his first thought was that it was a bomb. He quickly told my grandmother what happened and hung up the phone. Announcements came over the speakerphone that a small plane had hit the upper floors, and people should remain in their offices. My father went into the main area of his office where a small crowd of his co-workers were gathered around a screen. The screen was connected to video cameras that showed the outside of the building. What they saw shocked them. Just a few floors above them there were flames of fire and thick black smoke pouring out of the building. They unanimously decided to leave the building despite the orders to stay where they were.

When they stepped out into the hallway, they were confronted by a frightening scene. Parts of the hall were on fire, and the smoke was rapidly spreading. They quickly began the long trip down 77 flights of stairs. The smoke was thick, debris was falling, yet no one was panicking. They calmly reassured each other, while continuing to descend the crowded staircases. At one point the lights went out so they continued the rest of the descent in total darkness. Every so often there was some light from the firemen's flashlights. These firemen were heading upstairs, unknowingly to their death. On the way down, my father witnessed many terrifying sights — people on fire, collapsed hallways, indescribable scenes. When he reached the 30th floor (approximately) he thought his life was at an end. The building suddenly began shaking and swaying violently. The staircase twisted wildly. His life flashed before his eyes. He thought he would never be able to see his family again. There was nothing to do except to continue to try to get down.

After an hour and 20 minutes of descending staircase after staircase, my father finally reached the bottom. As he came out my father expected to see the same sunlight and clear blue sky that he had seen upon entering the building that morning. Instead he got another shock. It felt like he had entered a war zone. White ash and debris covered the street for blocks around. There were blown-up cars and overturned vehicles. Police cars and ambulances were smashed and destroyed. He heard crashing sounds coming from around the building every few seconds. He was standing in a foot of rubble staring around in confusion and searching for his co-workers. Rescuers began to shout, "Run!"

My father turned and ran. Exactly 4 minutes after he exit-
ed the building it collapsed. The mighty Twin Towers, which
had taken years to build, had disappeared in a matter of min-
utes!

My father kept on running. A tremendous cloud of smoke
seemed to chase him. He reached the bridge. He walked across
along with hundreds of other people escaping the city. At the end
of the bridge he got a ride home with a Jewish man who was
offering rides to people.

On that day when wives became widows, children became
orphans and many friends and relatives were lost, I was fortu-
nate enough to see my father return home safely. Baruch
Hashem — it was a true miracle!

Since this miracle, my father's life has changed forever. He no
longer looks at the world in the same way as before. He is con-
stantly thinking, what does Hashem want from him? He now
lives with this question every day and strives to be the best Jew
he can be.

This miracle has made me appreciate my father and life in
general so much more. Every moment is precious, and you never
know which moment might be your last. Make each moment
count and value each day. They are all invaluable.

Esther Malka Jankelowitz

❦

Roadsigns

As you travel to a new destination it is reassuring when you see
a sign on the highway that indicates you are going in the right direction. When you turn off at the exit ramp you may see another sign
pointing out the avenue you need. Perhaps the directions tell you to
pass the next three traffic lights before turning onto the correct lane.
If you find the exact lane you'll feel happy and relieved — you have
almost reached the destination. The last thing you have to do is go
down this lane and make a right turn at the next street. The fifth
house on this specific street is your friend's house.

While traveling on the road of life, it's important, as well as help-ful, to have accurate signs to follow. You need visual stimuli to help remind you that you are capable of excelling and to indicate the cor-rect path. Positive statements that you keep in your mind's eye are constant reminders of your potential and abilities.

Thought Starters

Nagging. Nagging is the voice inside telling you to clear the table. At the same time, you wonder, wasn't it perfectly empty just an hour ago? Nagging is the worries about many different things that trouble you. At the same time you wonder, "Can I control these problems?" Nagging is when you have doubts: "I am working so hard; perhaps it's too hard. Will I succeed?" They are the thoughts that bring you down and cause you to lose confidence. Nagging worries chase away your smile. These doubts, negative thoughts and worries can lead to frustration and self-doubt. The slightest thing can throw you off bal-ance. Because you want to get everything just right you're behaving all wrong. At such moments you need an emergency thought starter.

When it's hard to keep going and you think you'll explode, the advertisers tell you to reach for a coke or a cookie. If your waistline can't afford all those cookies, why not reach for a pos-itive thought instead? You may be asking, "How?" We all know that when you most need a positive thought, your mind goes blank. I got this idea when Basy said, "I have a collection of my favorite clippings from the *Yated*. They are taped inside my kitchen cabinet and they remind me to cheer up when I'm feel-ing dragged down."

When you read an inspiring Torah concept, copy it. Look for humorous and energizing thoughts or for a saying that helps you look at your problem from a lighter perspective. Begin by collect-ing clippings, sayings, cartoons, and photographs that bring a smile to your face. Tape them in strategic places where you are likely to see them at the most hectic times. Your new hangings do not have to cause clutter. If you like organization or are artistical-ly inclined, you might consider mounting your collection cre-atively, or even setting aside one wall of your room for display.

The important thing is that the uplifting thoughts you need will be right at hand.

A peak moment is a time in your life when you did something exceptionally well: it includes the jubilation that accompanied it. If you have a photograph of yourself at a peak moment, this is a perfect helpful stimulus for your room. Otherwise, you can capture the feeling with a written description or by framing a memento from the occasion. Have you seen a framed dollar bill in a local store? Business owners frequently frame and hang the first dollar they ever made when their store opened.

We decided to start immediately on this project at the workshop. Here are some examples from the workshop participants. I hope they will help you get started on your journey of self-discovery. What encouraging thoughts do you repeat to yourself when you feel overwhelmed?

Inspirational Decorating

True Responses:

When I was born in Russia, the hospital had a strict policy: The mother had to remain in the hospital for a week in total isolation. No phone calls or visits were allowed. My mother smuggled a tiny piece of paper to my father. In it she described how I looked and listed a few things she needed. My father saved that note all these years and gave it to me. I often look at it. At the time it was just a little piece of paper. Now its value cannot be described.

‿∂∾

Writing is pleasant because it keeps images before you. You search in the pockets of your mind for precious memories and write them down. The words express your thoughts and feelings and remind you of the peak moments.

My 13-month-old daughter is wearing her first pair of shoes, baruch Hashem! She took her first steps three weeks ago. It began with that magic moment when she decided to let go of the table, sail off into the wide open space and take three courageous steps into my arms. To her delight, her four older siblings were all there to cheer for her and applaud her triumph. All that afternoon, her brothers and sisters practiced with her. One sibling stood a few feet away and the others cheered and clapped when she took three tiny steps. After a while she was not only increasing her steps, but, as she walked, she applauded herself. In her young mind, walking and clapping go together.

I watched my little one walking, smiling and clapping and asked myself, "What does it take for us adults to feel that we are a success? How many 'steps' do we have to take? How much do we have to accomplish before we applaud ourselves inside? Have we set up our lives in a way that makes elation difficult and discouragement almost inevitable?"

✺

Notes, Gifts and Cards of Appreciation
From Friends and Colleagues

In this busy world, if someone takes the time to write and tell you how much he appreciates you, you know he means it. Keeping his words and gifts visible helps you acknowledge yourself once in a while too.

✺

I walked up the block and trudged up the stairs. I was glad to be home. As I opened the screen door I noticed a package. I let myself into the house and carried the box under my arm. I didn't take notice of it at first — I thought it couldn't possibly be for me.

I set down the box and went about my business. I started cooking supper for my family since my mother was at work. She wouldn't be home until later tonight. I knew there was a lot of homework so I took out my book and began. Then the phone rang. I talked for a while.

My mother came home. She seemed surprised to see the package sitting on the table — she had expected me to open it. "Did you look at this package?" she casually asked. Then a very wonderful thing occurred. I picked up the box, took a closer look and found out that it was addressed to me. I was so excited! I love receiving mail.

When I opened the box I found a ring and bracelet set inside. I shouted, "Hooray!" I couldn't believe this surprise gift was for me. It was beautiful. I checked the card in the box. It was a gift from my parents.

My mother explained that she appreciated that I always help out without being asked. Both of my parents decided to treat me to a present. I thanked my mother many times and told her that although it wasn't necessary I really enjoyed the gift. When my father came home I thankfully exclaimed, "This was the best surprise gift of my life!"

Suri A.

❧

I suppose you've had a busy day today. There are so many things that had to be done. Yet you still managed to squeeze time into your schedule to help your parents. When your mother thanks you, don't simply shrug your shoulders; pause and think about what you've done. Take a moment to look back on your day — your hours in school, your friends and teachers, and now the time you are spending with your family. The good feeling that you give to your parents when you offer to help without being asked makes them feel appreciated. It's important to realize the power of the little things you do. If you can absorb deep within yourself the importance of being gracious and helping others, you will achieve great things.

❧

Many teens shared stories about people they know well who have risen to the challenge of coping with a disability. There is a common theme in these stories. Unlike what we might expect, many people with a disability maintain a courageous and cheerful disposition. It makes me wonder why we can't take our problems, which are surely less significant, in stride. We all face emotional and intellectual challenges. These heroes can give us an important lesson on overcoming difficulties with grace and courage.

●✦ *The Perfect Mommy*

"Mommy is glad Hashem made her handicapped because that is how He wanted it and He knows best," says little Chany. Ari wisely adds, "If she didn't have cerebral palsy, she wouldn't always be home to spend time with us and tell us interesting stories."

My cousins expressed these thoughts about their mother, my aunt. My aunt was born in a sterile hospital in Rumania. The doctor who assisted in her delivery applied additional pressure to the undeveloped part of her brain on top of her head, causing severe damage to the motor section of the cerebrum. Quite a number of children whose birth was assisted by this doctor were born with cerebral palsy.

Cerebral palsy is a general term for a variety of disorders caused by damage to the brain. The damage occurs before or during birth or in the first few years of life. The damage may cause severe crippling or the symptoms may be so mild that they hardly interfere with the person's activities. Common effects of cerebral palsy are clumsy walking, lack of balance, shaking, jerky movements and unclear speech.

My Aunt Sarah has a keen mind and is an exceptional writer. She received scholarships throughout her high school and college years. However, there are many perfectly ordinary activities that she cannot perform. As she commented about her son, "It was hard for me to visualize that this totally helpless infant would grow up one day. He would take his own temperature, fasten his own buttons and also help me with mine, and pour a drink for both of us." We should appreciate our ability to perform simple actions, such as fastening buttons.

Treatment of cerebral palsy is aimed at preventing the worsening of symptoms and helping the person use his or her abilities to the best advantage. Each patient needs individual care and therapy.

Sarah was born in Rumania. She then traveled through Hungary, resided in Israel for a few years, toured France, settled in Canada and then moved permanently to the U.S. During all these numerous changes, the essential treatment that my aunt received was love. Most of her upbringing was in a quaint little home in Toronto. It was nestled in a quiet corner of town surrounded by cheerful daffodils and swaying evergreens. She was sent to the top schools in the country. Unfortunately, there were no Jewish institutions catering to individuals with this handicap. Although Sarah never received a proper Jewish education she is frum and has remained faithful to her religion. During her school years she met my uncle, who became her partner for life. They have two beautiful children.

The doctors were baffled when she had her first child. Having children was considered a great miracle. She says, "I held my baby in my arms for the first time. Thus my status as the child's mother was observed by the doctors, nurses and parents in the area. I felt confident as I held my son against my shoulder. In my tuneless voice I sang Shalom Aleichem to my infant to introduce him to Shabbos." While staying in the hospital she remembered no pain; she was overcome by the beauty and splendor of bearing a child. Yet she was emotionally burdened by the knowledge that she wouldn't be able to care for her own child.

Marie was hired to care for their firstborn son, Ari. "Feeding, burping, diapering, dressing, bathing and cuddling my baby were tasks performed by Marie, by my husband and by other members of my supportive family." Sarah felt helpless. A strange woman was able to caress her baby while she looked on. She repressed these sad thoughts because she believed with optimism that Hashem was guiding the world.

One sunny afternoon, her nurse had left and her husband was out shopping. The baby was napping. Suddenly she heard his insistent call. "I found the little cherub standing up in his crib and in need of a diaper change." Yet changing this child's diaper was a feat that required nimble dexterity and little Ari was always on the move.

The young mother prepared a bag for disposal and laid out five wipes for the fateful diaper change. With a rapidly beating heart she reached in and grasped the little boy and hoisted him out of the crib. His weight was too much for her and mother and son fell backwards onto the bed. Her pulse raced at the thought of what could have happened — she could have crushed her child. Being the determined person that she is, she continued with the task. About 10 minutes later the struggle was over. The wide-eyed toddler stared at his clumsy mother and a disarranged Pamper clung to his little bottom. The dazed yet triumphant mother regarded her little son with a love she had never felt before.

Only two and a half years later, Chanie was born. This daughter developed from an innocent, helpless preschooler into a beautiful, loving and loyal young adult. She and her brother were brought up in a warm and loving environment. They learned from their mother to observe the beauty and goodness in Hashem's world.

There were some bumps and potholes along the road. Yet they overcame them and remained a close family supported by their great and steady pillar, their mother Sarah.

My father answered some questions about his sister Sarah:

QUESTION: How did you cope with your sister's handicap?

ANSWER: She spent most of the year in special schools. At home she was treated with love and care like any other child.

QUESTION: Did you ever feel different because of having such a relation?

ANSWER: Of course not! She's my sister! We were all treated equally. Sarah was the same as the rest of us. She went wherever we went.

QUESTION: When you think of your sister's struggle what sticks out most in your mind?

ANSWER: What's astounding is that although she spent many years in a gentile environment she remained steadfast in her faith and in all aspects of *Yiddishkeit*.

QUESTION: Do you recall any incidents regarding Sarah?

ANSWER: Yes, I do remember when my parents were contemplating immigrating to America. We children were sworn to secrecy. However, it was Sarah who announced it to the whole neighborhood. My parents were worried about Sarah being accepted into the U.S. Only healthy people were allowed entry. When we went to the Canadian consul to get visas, Levi (my uncle) began playing with a little girl. The officials assumed this was my sister and immediately gave us our visas.

QUESTION: How did your sister meet her husband?

ANSWER: She was in a summer camp and he was a non-*frum* volunteer working there. Being a *frum* girl she faithfully *davened* each day and dressed modestly. He saw the beauty of *Yiddishkeit* and became *frum* because of her. By then he had decided he wanted to marry her. With the Rebbe's consent, the match was made.

QUESTION: What type of personality does your sister maintain?

ANSWER: She is remarkable. She is always optimistic, never depressed and always the peacemaker.

Reading about Sarah for the umpteenth time still brings tears to my eyes. Simple everyday actions are constant struggles for her. By contemplating an ordinary day that she lives through I have learned to appreciate the simple things in life. You may grumble or gripe about walking to school on a wintry day while this woman wishes she could simply grasp a cup and sip her coffee with ease.

The wonder of it all is that she is accepting of her disorder. She never seems embittered or in bad spirits. When people gawk, she smiles, and when they make biting comments, she laughs it off. The way she handles her handicap causes us to view her as we would any-one else. She is one of the most special people in my life. Everyone should aspire to come close to her level.

Chanie N.

Gems on a Chain

She sat at the seashore building a sandcastle. First she dug a deep hole. Then she carefully mixed the sand with water until it was not too hard and not too soft. She used three different-size cups to form towers, packing the cups with sand and carefully turning them over. Sometimes the tower crumbled and she had to try again. Finally things started to take shape and looked lovely. The castle had roads leading up to it. Twig "trees" framed the castle and windows were carved out in neat rows. Its ten towers rose proudly to the sky. She smiled happily. She got up to look for a scrap of something that could be used for the flag. She hadn't noticed that the ocean was mysteriously coming toward her castle as the sun began to get lower in the sky. She was absorbed in her search.

There it was. A pretty napkin in the food bag would make a perfect flag. Her mother said she could have it. She even found a Popsicle stick and pushed it through the napkin. It looked almost like a flag. Eagerly she ran back to the castle. She hadn't seen the wave come. Where was her castle? All that remained was a muddy mess and some twig trees lying in a heap.

You expected things to be a certain way. You made plans and you focused all your faculties on achieving the desired outcome. You planned carefully because you wanted to be in control and organized. Perfection is very important to you. You want every detail to be flawless.

A minor disturbance upsets your careful plans. Little things occur differently than you anticipated. Sometimes your emotions are so intense that you can't contain them. Your face may even look different. Your eyes appear sad and you may need some quiet.

What do you do when you don't know what to do?

Do negative thoughts come at you out of nowhere and hit you like a wave?

Does this mean that you are a failure?

Is the successful person one who copes well when everything goes smoothly?

Perhaps the successful person is someone who is able to be flexible. You can choose to float on that wave instead of sinking. It's important to be able to adapt well to new situations. This will help you achieve a more complete and satisfying life. You will be able to solve practical problems, develop insight into others, improve your relationships, and reach your goals.

As I'm writing these words, my 1-year-old baby is sitting in the doorway. It's an exciting challenge to squeeze in a paragraph or two before she requests my attention. She has pulled off both her socks. I can see her toes and she's saying, "Ah, nah, ah, bah." How much time will I have to write before she demands that I pick her up? How did I ever complete the last five books? They weren't written under perfect conditions. I have to be determined and flexible. When I have a free moment I pick up a pen and scribble a few lines. When I have a free half hour I rush to the computer. Many times the baby wakes up just as I've really begun to concentrate and make progress. I'm interrupted and I begin again when I can. I continue to try different techniques and to see what will work. I can't count the number of times I am interrupted, but I don't give up, and little by little the book takes shape.

You have to be flexible and adapt to the situation at hand. Last year everyone enjoyed my new book that came out for Chanukah. In order to meet that deadline I spent hours entering corrections with a 1-month-old baby on my lap. I never would have imagined that I'd spend my maternity leave from teaching typing a few hours each day.

Rebbetzin Esther Greenberg said, "A person who knows how to direct his inner dialogue in a constructive and positive way can gain tremendous achievement in personality development." We have a choice when we are faced with a seemingly impossible situation. We don't have to feel despair. We can find a way to turn the situation into something positive. I learned about adapting to thorny situations from many different teachers. I heard a story about a young girl who was almost blind. In order to test her vision, her mother asked her to form a necklace out of a collection of beads. Ariella was stuck because she couldn't possibly fulfill the request. Her vision was too poor for the task. Yet she didn't want to simply tell her mother, "I can't do this," because she knew that it would cause her mother pain.

"Sort them according to color," her mother requested, "then the necklace will be a beautiful one." Ariella sat and fiddled with the beads. Her mother didn't realize that she couldn't see any colors at all any longer. She could barely make out the bead's blurry outline. How would she arrange these beads on the string? She imagined that some of the beads were happy and some were sad. It's important to put the happy ones near the sad ones. This would give the sad beads courage and hope. Ariella concluded, "If you put a happy person near a sad person, the happy one can bring joy to those around her. I'm surrounded by people who are sad because of my condition, I will be the happy person who will give others courage and hope. I may not see well with my eyes but I can see in a way that really matters — with my mind." As Ariella groped for the beads and made the best necklace she could form, a profound idea came to her.

Ariella decided to create a second chain of unique gems. These gems would not be diamonds or pearls or even colored beads. Her gems would be Torah values such as faith, happiness, contentment, kindheartedness, prayer and enthusiasm. Although Ariella is blind she captures hopeful images through song. Each gem — positive feeling — is expressed in a different song. You hear the overwhelming happiness in her laughter and the lively tunes she sings and you feel uplifted. I can listen to these songs over and over again. Someone who can't even see created this wonderful music.

There is always a hopeful image somewhere. The important thing is not to let trouble stop you. Don't let your problems direct your life. Rather create and hold onto your own necklace of gems and feel connected to a higher goal.

Everyone can create her own necklace. Just gather precious thoughts one at a time. Write down the lessons that speak to you. They may be lessons from the Torah, stories about *tzaddikim* or lessons from people you know and admire. Think about these gems. Look at them and hold them close to you. Ask yourself how you can apply these ideals in real life. Don't lose them. Each lesson you absorb will connect in a chain. Hold on to your memories. They are your gems. They give you strength to grow.

How to Start Your "Necklace"

Think about what you like to do and with whom you like to do it. Once you have goals you will find opportunities. Goals lead to action.

1. Take 10 minutes to learn a Torah thought from a book that interests you because you want to do it. Homework doesn't count.

2. Don't waste a minute. While you walk down the street or wait on line you can think about those images that inspired you this week. Review what's important to you

3. R' Avigdor Miller said, "Remember that the *Shechinah* is everywhere around you. When you see the face of a fellow Jew remember that the *Shechinah* shines from his face." Keep this in mind.

4. Make it a priority. There are so many distractions that make demands on our time. We have to decide to get rid of some of the clutter so that we can create time for what's truly important.

❧ *Escorting Eli*

I was introduced to Eli when I was in eleventh grade. I accepted the position of being a Bnos Chavivos escort. I thought it would be a quick and easy mitzvah. I'd walk an adorable 8-year-old boy to Bnos every Shabbos. I looked forward eagerly to our first Shabbos walk together. I had no idea what was in store for me.

I arrived 5 minutes early and knocked on the door. A bubbly, adorable, 8-year-old boy came bouncing out of the house and planted a wet kiss on my face. "Chani Geller, right," he said with a grin. He cheerfully waved good-bye to his mother and we were immediately on our way.

I told him all about my family and asked him about his family. Although his speech was a bit slurred, he had great verbal skills, a relatively good vocabulary and great dramatic flair. It took us about 20 minutes to walk from 41st Street and 15th Avenue to 49th Street and 14th Avenue. That was a reasonable amount of time considering the distance. As we walked, Eli greeted just about every passerby. We had kept an amiable conversation going. I really enjoyed myself. We were off to a good start.

When I arrived at Bnos the head leaders looked at their watches with an astonished look on their faces. They explained that Eli had never been on time to Bnos before in his life. He would usually stop somewhere along the way and refuse to walk any further. I assured them that I hadn't done anything unusual. They figured that Eli had matured over the summer. Perhaps this year things would be different.

For seven days I comforted myself with this theory and didn't worry about our upcoming outing. Unfortunately it wasn't that simple. On the second week as soon as we reached the corner of his block Eli sat down on the sidewalk. He refused to continue. I tried reminding him of all the fun and nosh that he was missing at Bnos. I complimented him on how good he'd been the previous week and how impressed I was. This was all in vain. Eli wasn't interested. I tried sitting down with him and then having a race to see who could get up first. I finally ran away from him saying, "You can't catch me!" and Eli jumped up to chase after me. We were on our way again.

After he had caught me I quickly began telling Eli the story of the Parashah to distract him. This worked for a while and Eli walked agreeably for five or six blocks. On 47th Street, Eli sat down again. I tried the "catch me" game that had worked so well before, but this time he wasn't interested. Since we were standing at a crossing light I offered to let him be my professional crossing guard. When the sign changed he would tell me to go. This worked. I noticed that Eli generally stood up to challenges.

This week it took us 45 minutes to get there. Eli gave me a grand good-bye hug and ran inside. The Bnos leaders looked at me sympathetically. We were 20 minutes late.

On the third week I thought of a new game we could play. I explained the rules to Eli. He could choose any corner to stop at but we'd only stop at two corners. If he stopped at a corner we'd count to 100 together and then he'd have to get up and continue walking. If he didn't jump up immediately the rule was that we'd only count to 50 the next time he stopped. It worked. Eli would jump up immediately and he only stopped at two corners. He seemed to feel mature being the one in charge of counting and having the choice of where to stop.

One week I noticed an unfamiliar man watching us. I warily counted with Eli, hoping the method would work again. Baruch Hashem, it did, and as soon as Eli began walking he too noticed the man. He ran over to give his father a kiss. I was glad his father hadn't seen me having difficulties.

I continued escorting Eli the following year. Eli has matured. Our second year is different. He hardly stops anymore. As we walk he enjoys identifying letters and small words.

One week Eli had a new stunt. As soon as he was certain that his mother was safely back in the house, Eli bent over and rolled up his pants. He wanted everyone to see his new Shabbos shoes. This was his very first pair of Shabbos shoes.

Toward Purim I began taking Eli and his younger Down Syndrome brother out together. Eli walked ahead like a mature 20 year old, giving Raffi instructions along the way. When Raffi sat down on the sidewalk, he'd say, "Raffi, let's see if you can catch me." If Raffi ignored him he'd say, "When I say 100 you must stand up." If Raffi still sat he'd gently pull him up. It was adorable to watch Eli in his big brother mode.

On our expeditions to Bnos Chavivos, Eli rarely stopped anymore. I continuously complimented him on his maturity. I once told him that when he was a "little boy" he had done the same things as Raffi was doing. He thought that was hysterical and he laughed heartily. Naturally Eli made sure to live up to my *compliments. We had no more need for games like follow the leader, boxes or tag. Our days of making a spectacle of ourselves were over.*

I met Eli this year with his new escort. Was he the same Eli? He walked along making polite conversation and behaving like a gentleman. I think of all the "fun" his new escort has missed and I breathe a sigh of relief. I feel triumphant. I have really made a difference. My energy and toil weren't for naught.

Sometimes we gain more from an experience when we lower our original expectations. It's important never to give up and to always keep trying to accomplish our ultimate goal.

Chani G.

Standing Tall

The woman I interviewed is a giant in generosity, courage and a cheerful disposition despite her dwarfed appearance. Dwarfism is a condition that a person is born with. His or her height usually does not exceed four feet, even after surgical intervention. People with kidney disease are usually affected with dwarfism as well, and it just leads to double pain for them.

The woman I interviewed is 24 and married to a *frum*, healthy, tall man. She is the mother of an adorable 2-year-old daughter. This is what she told me:

When I was born, I had a transplant immediately. Baruch Hashem, it was successful and I am perfectly healthy, other than my height. This is a tremendous blessing. At the age of 12 we — my mother and I — began investigating different aspects of surgery so that I could possibly grow taller.

There were many complications involved in the surgery — like having to be in a wheelchair for two years and the excruciating pain of turning the screw in my legs every day of those two years.

Hardest of all, I had to learn how to walk again so as not to place too much weight on my fragile legs. We weighed all the options and decided to go ahead with it. It would be worth all the pain because I would hopefully grow to four feet. The surgery was performed and baruch Hashem it was really successful.

In elementary school I didn't have so many friends. Children can be that way. There are many adults who still don't bother to conceal their feelings when I first meet them. Once I got to high school, though, I made many wonderful friends, girls with whom I am extremely close even today, although we live on separate continents. For my wedding, my parents flew my closest friend to America. It's an expensive ticket to pay for on a kollel income but my parents wanted her to celebrate with me at my wedding.

When I was old enough to start thinking of marriage I established some rules. I didn't go out; we met in the house. I also requested that I speak to every prospective mate on the phone before we met in person. I realize that people really are taken aback by my appearance. They may be aware of what to expect but they are still surprised. I guess that Hashem has a master plan because I did not end up speaking to my husband on the phone beforehand. I vehemently refused to marry a dwarf because then the fate of my children would be sealed. If both parents are dwarfs the children will definitely be dwarfs. If only one is then they have as much chance of having children of normal height as anyone else.

I've spent enough time in hospitals so I can honestly say that after seeing all the other things that can go wrong in a person's body I am quite grateful. My handicap affects only my appearance. It does not affect my health and entire way of living. The only reason it's uncomfortable is because of people in the street and how they behave: The young boy who calls out, "Look at the little mother," to all who can hear as I pass. The teenage girls who smile sweetly at me and say a false hello might mean well but do not realize how degrading their tone of voice is. I recall visiting my aunt in her bungalow colony and I overheard a crowd of boys discussing me as if I weren't there. I was pushing my nephew on the swing and one of the boys just stood there staring at me with his mouth open as if I could not see him.

Here's what we ask of you. It's not a big favor. It's actually quite simple: Just be you. Treat us as you would regular people. Don't gape when we pass but don't turn in the other direction either. Most of all don't treat us like a mentally disabled child. Don't smile and say "Hi" in that condescending tone — would you greet a regular person in that way? That's exactly what we are — regular people.

A child laughs and the parents say nothing, or worse, they chuckle too. Why wouldn't the child continue such behavior if they see their parents' reaction? Please don't pile more burdens on someone who already has to suffer more than his share.

I know that I am blessed. I lead a regular life. A lot of this is due to my mother's constant, wonderful support. My mother was extremely compassionate and encouraging. She always pushed me to do things I would have hesitated to do because of my appearance. She instilled in me the confidence to withstand the stares or worse. I'm sure people aren't mean on purpose, it's just ignorance. It was also my mother who encouraged me to share my story with others. I hope they will hear and be inspired. I also want to tell people, don't give up! Don't despair! Hashem will help you overcome your problems as He has helped me. I hope people will perhaps change their outlook toward others like me.

⋙⋘

Count your garden by the flowers,
Never by the leaves that fall.
Count your days by the golden hours,
Don't remember clouds at all.
Count the night by stars, not shadows,
Count your life by smiles, not tears.
And with joy on every birthday,
Count your age by friends, not years.

Anonymous

✦ REMEMBERING YANKY

I stood in the chapel. Tears rolled down my cheeks as I remembered my family friend, Yanky Eisen, a"h. As I stood there rooted to my spot, I could not help but remember the positive memories our families had shared.

Yanky was my role model. He was a young boy who always had a smile on his face. He was described in an article written about him as "full of life." Due to Canavan's Disease, Yanky could not walk, talk or communicate like other children, but he taught us the value of life. We remember Yanky and his infectious laughter and contagious giggles. His mega-watt smile, as described by two of his counselors, "never failed to change your day."

His parents considered Yanky their miracle. Their endless love, affection and patience inspired me. I could never forget their optimistic and humorous approach to life. Despite the knowledge that Yanky's illness was ultimately fatal, they treasured each day. The whole day revolved around Yanky: What will he eat? Is he comfortable? How can we make Yanky laugh? Yanky's father, Shaul, had approaches that were so funny that they even made me laugh. Fraidy, Yanky's mother, displayed boundless love. She inspired me. I hope one day to nurture my children like she did. On one of his last days, the doctor said that he had lived so long (until 15 years) because of the careful attention his parents had given him. Children with Canavan's Disease usually live up to 10 years.

Canavan's Disease is a relatively rare but always fatal inherited degenerative brain disorder that primarily affects children of Ashkenazi descent. There is no cure for the disease. Symptoms include lack of head control and abnormal muscle tone such as stiffness and floppiness. The children therefore cannot walk, sit or talk.

Yanky attended Camp HASC every summer from when he was a young child. He charmed everyone and radiated love to all his counselors, thus allaying his parents' concern about the newness of the experience and his temporary separation from them. One of his counselors noted that it was Yanky who inspired him with a passion to enter the field of Special Education. Often his counselors visited him in his home after *the summer camp session. "Yanky's positive energy was pala-pable. It alleviated any stress that occurred during the day."*

Whenever I visited Yanky, I would first go over to give him a kiss and try to make him laugh. Dolcey, his helper, often commented on our friendliness to Yanky, but we only did it out of love and admi-ration for him.

I asked Fraidy, Yanky's mother, to share some of her memo-ries of Yanky:

ESTY: How did you find out about Yanky's illness?

FRAIDY: When Yanky was 6 months old he didn't do what other children his age do. He didn't hold his head up or reach for things like a bottle. I began going from doctor to doctor. Then we found out that Yanky has Canavan's Disease. At that time only thirty children in the U.S. had it.

ESTY: How did you react to the news?

FRAIDY: I cried for two days. Then Shaul and I decided to make the best possible world for Yanky. We decided to live every day to the fullest and enjoy him. We were determined to enjoy every day that Yanky lived.

ESTY: In what way did Yanky's having Canavan's help others?

FRAIDY: We were able to help scientists find a way to prevent Canavan's Disease. The scientists took my gene, Shaul's and Yanky's and isolated it. They then figured out a way to pre-vent Canavan's.

ESTY: Do you know anyone else with a child that has this disease?

FRAIDY: Yes, we know a family in South Africa. Their child is a bit younger than Yanky was.

ESTY: How did you cope with Yanky on a day-to-day basis?

FRAIDY: I just devoted myself to him and lived one day at a time. Yanky felt our love and he responded.

ESTY: Is it true that Yanky would refrain from making noises so that he shouldn't wake you up in the morning?

FRAIDY: Yes. When I got up in the morning and went to his crib. I often found that Yanky was awake. His eyes were wide open but he hadn't made a sound so as not to wake us.

ESTY: Are there ways that people can help families with handicapped children?

FRAIDY: A friend has an autistic child. She complained that many people don't come to help because they don't know how to deal with him. I personally didn't have any problems because Yanky attracted people to him. People wanted to interact with Yanky because of his cheerful nature, but I could see that some people do have problems with this.

ESTY: What have you done in Yanky's memory?

FRAIDY: A *Sefer Torah* is being written in Yanky's memory.

If you have the opportunity to become associated with a handicapped child don't hold back. Use your gifts from Hashem and get to know them. Be helpful in every way. It may be difficult at first, but trust me — you'll never regret it. You will get to see the inner beauty of every child. Every child is created in Hashem's image.

Esty Neumann

$\backsim\!\!\sim\!\!\backsim$

*N*o *matter what the situation is, something good can result from it. Hashem gives you extra strength to do something beneficial. The past year was filled with difficult situations, challenges and hardships. However, every student in the school tried to do something about it. Each person resolved to work in a different area. Before we go to sleep we should think about the day that just passed. Did we improve and correct something today? There are halachos posted in the halls. These are our goals for the following week.*

Hardships, challenges and difficulties cause some people to break and others to break records. Each person can find talents and strengths they didn't know they had. The situation may be difficult but we can still rise above it.

Leah Malka F.

❧ Just Like Me as I Am

Her emaciated legs barely carried her. She wore an oversized dress supported by weak, slumped shoulders. Her young face was a ghostly white and her colorless cheeks were sunken. Her hair — could it be? Was she actually wearing a wig? Oh. She was one of those. One of those struck by the dreaded illness.

The boy passed by quickly and looked the other way.

He sat there in his wheelchair. It had a cushion to support his quivering head. He couldn't confine his tongue inside his mouth and saliva dribbled on his chin. His limbs were fastened to the wheelchair. Oh. He was one of those. One of those suffering from the dreaded disease, cerebral palsy.

A passerby stopped to take a look and then sighed with pity.

They walked together, the young woman and her dog. The dog, her instrument of vision. She seemed to be gazing at the dark void ahead of her, her sightless eyes almost completely hidden by her large sunglasses. She clutched the dog's leash. Must she rely on a dog's vision in bright daylight? Oh. She was one of those.

The onlooker watched, bewildered.

What an awful disability! I'm not referring to a physical handicap. What I'm referring to is our inability to see. Why are we unable to see their pain? What handicap prevents us from understanding, loving and accepting? Do you see beyond the wheelchair? The wig? The guide dog? Try to see — a person, a heart and soul, a person just like you and me.

Lately I have become closely acquainted with a 7-year-old boy named Chaim — a victim of spina bifida. He is accepting and proud. He accepts help graciously, yet certainly tries not to take advantage of his situation. He is careful to keep up with his schoolwork, even though that requires additional effort.

Rather than bemoan his inability to run and skip with his friends in school, he creates a different kind of fun. I watched my 7-year-old brother, Hershy, race him countless times. Chaim calls out, "Look everyone, look how quickly I can crawl across the hall!" Seeing his great excitement, Hershy joins him on all fours and the race is on! Surprisingly, the winning athlete is Chaim.

Chaim doesn't consider himself different or inferior to his peers. He moved his black yarmulke to the side and a lump on his small head was exposed.

"Do you know what this is, Devoiry? This is my shunt. Do you have a shunt?"

Do I have a shunt? He asked the question with the same tone one would ask a friend, "Do you have blue eyes?" I was quite taken aback. Yet as I thought about it, I realized that Chaim had taught me a great lesson. Just as Hashem gave him large, dark, curious eyes, Hashem created him with an open spine.

The shunt drains the water above his brain. The water then runs through tubes down his front. Chaim ran my fingers down his chest. "Look, you can feel my tubes," he said. Indeed, they were quite noticeable. I was curious if he knew the tubes' function. I asked him. His response was, "What do you mean? Everyone has tubes!" I thought about it. He's right. Everyone does have tubes — all sorts of veins and arteries run through our body. Who are we to decide that our tubes are normal and his aren't?

Chaim attracts attention without meaning to. He is very small and underweight and he walks with metal crutches which are about two feet each. I assumed that he knew that he was different. One day he came home with a gold yarmulke that he had received from the busdriver. I suggested that he shouldn't wear it to yeshivah. "You don't want to look different, Chaim," I explained. I was afraid that his classmates would tease him if he wore a gold yarmulke. His response was, "I'm already different than everyone else." My heart fell. I was afraid to hear the rest. He continued, "I have different eyes, a different nose, different ears …"

Let's take a lesson from Chaim. Let's learn to appreciate all that we were blessed with. Chaim, a 7-year-old boy, cannot run and play with his friends. In his short life he has learned how to make the most of his situation. We who can run, jump, climb stairs and dance without a second thought should at least be grateful and not take these things for granted. We should surely relate to the handicapped with respect and tenderness.

Devoiry S.

❧ Stuck on the Palisades

It was an ordinary summer day around six years ago. My family was on the way home from the country. We had been visiting my sister in camp. As we were driving down the Palisades Parkway, we heard a loud honking noise. We turned and saw a man in the car beside us frantically pointing at our tire. My father pulled over to the side of the road, got out of the car and looked at the tire. The tire was flat and the treads were rolling along with the traffic. We had a spare tire in the car. My father attempted to change the tire but the old tire refused to come off. Unfortunately we were stuck on the side of the Palisades.

It was getting dark. My mother was home in the city, so my oldest sister took charge. Many Jewish families whom we didn't recognize offered their help, however, no one could get the tire to come off. A kind man insisted on bringing us to his sister's home nearby.

Our family arrived at the house of the Shteif family. The kind man then called for a tow truck to pick up our car. Meanwhile we were served a delicious supper. My little sister was placed in a comfortable bed while the rest of us played with all of the family's toys. They treated us as if we had known them for years; they were unbelievable. My father returned with our fixed car a short while later. After thanking them again and again, we were on our way home.

This act of kindness to total strangers was amazing. They helped us change our moments of despair to utmost pleasure. No matter who is in trouble, there are always Jews who will help him triumph. There is no other nation in the world that cares for each other to this extent. Who is like the Jewish nation?

Chani J.

❧

One of the gifts one may receive while going through a difficult situation is finding new friends. People who were strangers before show love and kindness and go out of their way to help you. They make you feel that you have known them for years. As Chani concludes, "Who is like the Jewish nation?"

❦

Students spend at least half of their waking life in school. That's a lot of time to spend doing something unless it makes us happy. So many students complain about school. They dread waking up in the morning and going to their classroom. Many girls feel that they have no choice, "And that's it."

Part of the problem is that we often have a rigid picture of what kind of learning one can feel excited about. It's not the teacher who makes your day exciting — it's you. You can make your experience in school a more positive one by infusing it with your interest and involvement. Every day you can ask yourself, "What have I learned today?" You may gain insight from a teacher, a fellow student or the staff in the office. In addition to scholastic advancement there are other important experiences in school — social, spiritual and practical. Seek and you will find.

❧ *Don't Quit!*

We were in the fifth grade. The class was reading aloud from their literature books. My teacher had called on me to read. I mispronounced a word in the first sentence and another word in the next. My class laughed at both of my mistakes since they were both words that everyone knows. How can one read "great" as "greet"?

My class laughed for the second time and for the second time my face turned scarlet. My teacher ignored the class and spoke to me. "Continue," she said, as if I had just stopped reading for no reason. I finished reading the page without any other mistakes.

After I finished, my teacher said, "Girls, I want you all to learn from this. Sometimes you will make a mistake and people will laugh at you. Although it may seem hard for you to continue, it is important to do so. This way you will show yourself and those who laughed at you that you can do it."

During that year I was frequently asked to read aloud. Sometimes I made mistakes. Now, whenever I feel like quitting, I remember this incident and it gives me the courage to continue. It has helped me do many things that seemed impossible at first.

Tova L.

⌒◡⌒

Most people *almost* keep practicing long enough to succeed. Most people *almost* hang in there long enough to learn a new skill. Most people *almost* have enough determination to win.

Chances are that you have a dream. There is a skill you wish you could learn. There may be an instrument you want to master. Your dreams are hidden inside you. They add spice to your life and give others satisfaction and joy.

It's difficult in the beginning. You need persistence. You may feel like giving up after your first music or dance lesson. When you feel like giving up, promise yourself to hang in there one more week, or one more month. No one is remarkable at playing an instrument when they begin. You must have realistic expectations. Persevere — you may be pleasantly surprised.

Learn how to do new things for *yourself*. Don't worry if others will like it. What's important is that *you* want to do it.

Why do some people seize the opportunity? Why do others pass it up with a sigh? Another obstacle is procrastination. We often spend months and years waiting for the right time. We put our dreams aside until the time comes when we won't be as busy as we are now. The "right time" might never come. We have to decide that the right time is right *now*.

Everyone can't do everything well. However, we can all do much more than we had originally thought possible.

A Note to the Reader

The main reason I have this page in here is so readers everywhere can share their thoughts, questions, ideas and stories. My teen readers have been the most enthusiastic writers. I will try my very best to respond.

Roiza Weinreich
625 Avenue L
Brooklyn, N.Y. 11230

❧

About the Author

Roiza Devorah Weinreich is the bestselling author of *There Will Never Be Another You, In Joy, A Happier You, W.H.A.T. Can Relieve Stress* and *A Gift for Teens*. Each book gives you the feeling that you are visiting with the author. There are questions, interviews, stories and exercise pages to help you feel that you are a participant in a workshop as you read the book. Roiza has designed and presented practical workshops based on Torah principles and true success stories for fifteen years. She is a teacher at Bais Yaakov High School. She also speaks at school and *tzedakah* gatherings.

This volume is part of
THE ARTSCROLL SERIES®
an ongoing project of
translations, commentaries and expositions
on Scripture, Mishnah, Talmud, Halachah,
liturgy, history, the classic Rabbinic writings,
biographies and thought.

For a brochure of current publications
visit your local Hebrew bookseller
or contact the publisher:

Mesorah Publications, ltd

4401 Second Avenue
Brooklyn, New York 11232
(718) 921-9000
www.artscroll.com